The Excellence of Fasting & The Fasting Person's Conduct

Shaykh Muḥammad bin Sa'īd Raslān

ISBN: 978-1-6384-8056-3

First Edition: Shʿabān 1442 A.H. / April 2021 C.E.

Cover Design: Aljadeed Design Co.

Translation: Abdullah Imraan

Translation (Appendix): Abu Muhammad Mustapha Abdul Hakeem

Revision & Editing: Maktabatulirshad Staff

Typesetting & Formatting: Abū Sulaymān Muḥammad ʿAbdul-Azīm ibn Joshua Baker

Subject: Admonition/Fasting

Website: www.maktabatulirshad.com

Email: info@maktabatulirshad.com

مكتبة الإرشاد
Maktabatul-Irshad
PUBLICATIONS

المحتويات

TABLE OF CONTENTS

PERMISSION OF SHAYKH MUHAMMAD SAEED RASLAN TO TRANSLATE & PUBLISH SEVERAL BOOKS

بسم الله الرحمن الرحيم

الحمد لله وحده، والصلاة والسلام على من لا نبي بعده صلى الله عليه وسلم، وبعد:

فقد أذنت للأخ المكرم أبي سليمان محمد عبد العظيم بن بيكر صاحب مكتبة (الإرشاد للنشر والتوزيع) بمدينة غرسبورو بولاية (North Carolina) بالولايات المتحدة الأمريكية بطباعة ترجمة الكتب الآتية:

١- فضل الصيام وسلوك الصائمين. ٢- احرص على ما ينفعك.
٣- الأسماء والصفات أصل العلم. ٤- التصفية والتربية.
٥- حسن الخلق. ٦- لا تحزن. ٧- عداوة الشيطان.
٨- معنى تحقيق التوحيد. ٩- لماذا هي أعظم.
١٠- نعمة الزواج وجملة من آداب الزفاف.
١١- خطورة المخدرات والإدمان على الفرد والمجتمع.

وذلك لفضيلة الوالد أبي عبدالله محمد بن سعيد رسلان حفظه الله بحفظه الجميل.

أسأل الله أن يوفقه لما يحب ويرضى، وصلى الله وسلم على عبد الله ورسوله نبينا محمد صلى الله عليه وسلم.

وكتب

ابو محمد عبدالله بن محمد بن سعيد رسلان

سبك الأحد - أشمون - المنوفية - مصر

أبو محمد عبد الله بن محمد بن سعيد رسلان

٥/٤/٢٠٢١م - ٢٣ شعبان ١٤٤٢هـ.

أبو محمد عبد الله بن محمد بن سعيد رسلان

ومن يتوكل على الله فهو حسبه

١٤٢٢/٨/ هـ

بِسۡمِ ٱللَّهِ ٱلرَّحۡمَٰنِ ٱلرَّحِيمِ

All Praise belongs to Allāh alone. O Allāh! Elevate the rank upon the one whom there is no prophet to come after him. O Allāh! Bestow peace upon him.

To proceed:

I permit the honored brother, Abū Sulaymān Muḥammad ʿAbdul ʿAẓīm Baker, the owner of Maktabatulirshad Publications in Greensboro, North Carolina of the United States of America, to translate and publish the following books:

1. **The excellence of fasting & the conduct of the fasting person**
2. **Strive to that which is beneficial to you**
3. **The Names and Attributes of Allāh is the foundation for Religious Knowledge**
4. **Purification and Islāmic Nurturing**
5. **Excellent moral conduct**
6. **Don't grieve**
7. **Shaytān's Enmity**
8. **The meaning of actualizing Tawḥīd**
9. **Why is it the greatest**
10. **The bounty of Marriage and a series of etiquettes concerning the wedding feast**
11. **The danger of personal drug abuse, addiction, and the break down of the community**

This (permission) is granted on the part of the Noble Shaykh, our father, Abū ʿAbdullāh Muḥammad bin Saʿīd Raslan, May Allāh continue to preserve him.

I ask Allāh to grant him (i.e., the owner of Maktabatulirshad Publications) Tawfīq to everything Allāh loves and is pleased. May Allāh elevate His Messenger's rank and status, our Prophet Muḥammad, and May He grant him peace.

Written by:

Abū Muḥammad ʿAbdullāh bin Muḥammad Saʿīd Raslan

Subuk al-Ahad, Ashmoon, al-Munafiyyah Egypt

On 23rd Day of Shʿabān 1442 AH

TRANSLITERATION TABLE

Consonants

ء	ʾ	د	d	ض	ḍ	ك	k
ب	b	ذ	dh	ط	ṭ	ل	l
ت	t	ر	r	ظ	ẓ	م	m
ث	th	ز	z	ع	ʿ	ن	n
ج	j	س	s	غ	gh	هـ	h
ح	ḥ	ش	sh	ف	f	و	w
خ	kh	ص	ṣ	ق	q	ي	y

Vowels

Short	ـَ	a	ـِ	i	ـُ	u
Long	ـَا	ā	ـِي	ī	ـُو	ū
Diphthongs	ـَوْ	aw	ـَيْ	ay		

Arabic Symbols & their meanings

عَزَّ وَجَلَّ	(Allāh) the Mighty & Sublime
سُبْحَانَهُ وَتَعَالَى	Glorified & Exalted is Allāh
رَحِمَهُ اللَّهُ	May Allāh have mercy on him
حَفِظَهُ اللهُ	May Allāh preserve him
صَلَّى اللَّهُ عَلَيْهِ وَعَلَى آلِهِ وَسَلَّمَ	May Allāh elevate his rank & grant him peace
جَلَّ جَلَالُهُ	(Allāh) His Majesty is Exalted
جَلَّ وَعَلَا	(Allāh) the Sublime & Exalted
تَبَارَكَ وَتَعَالَى	(Allāh) the Blessed & Exalted
رَضِيَ اللَّهُ عَنْهُمْ	May Allāh be pleased with them
رَضِيَ اللَّهُ عَنْهَا	May Allāh be pleased with her
رَضِيَ اللَّهُ عَنْهُ	May Allāh be pleased with him
عَلَيْهِ الصَّلَاةُ وَالسَّلَامُ	May Allāh elevate his rank & grant him peace
رَحِمَهُمُ اللَّهُ	May Allāh have mercy upon them

INTRODUCTION

بِسْمِ ٱللَّهِ ٱلرَّحْمَٰنِ ٱلرَّحِيمِ

All Praise is due to Allāh. We thank Him, seek His assistance, and ask for His forgiveness. We seek refuge with Allāh from the evil of our souls and the wicked consequences of our actions. None can guide whomever Allāh allows to go astray, and none can mislead whomever Allāh guides. I testify that there is no Deity worthy of worship, in truth, except Allāh alone, Who has no partner. I also bear witness that Muḥammad (ﷺ) is His servant and Messenger. Allāh said:

﴿ يَٰٓأَيُّهَا ٱلَّذِينَ ءَامَنُوا۟ ٱتَّقُوا۟ ٱللَّهَ حَقَّ تُقَاتِهِۦ وَلَا تَمُوتُنَّ إِلَّا وَأَنتُم مُّسْلِمُونَ ١٠٢ ﴾

"O you who believe! Fear Allāh (by doing all that He has ordered and by abstaining from all that He has forbidden) as He should be feared. [Obey Him, be thankful to Him, and remember Him always], and die not except in a state of Islām (as Muslims) with complete submission to Allāh." [Sūrah ʿĀli ʿImrān (3):102] Shaykh Muḥammad bin Saʿīd Raslān

Allāh said:

﴿ يَٰٓأَيُّهَا ٱلنَّاسُ ٱتَّقُواْ رَبَّكُمُ ٱلَّذِى خَلَقَكُم مِّن نَّفۡسٖ وَٰحِدَةٖ وَخَلَقَ مِنۡهَا زَوۡجَهَا وَبَثَّ مِنۡهُمَا رِجَالٗا كَثِيرٗا وَنِسَآءٗ وَٱتَّقُواْ ٱللَّهَ ٱلَّذِى تَسَآءَلُونَ بِهِۦ وَٱلۡأَرۡحَامَۚ إِنَّ ٱللَّهَ كَانَ عَلَيۡكُمۡ رَقِيبٗا ١ ﴾

"O mankind! Be dutiful to your Lord, Who created you from a single person (Adam), and from him (Adam) He created his wife [Hawwa (Eve)]. From them both, He created many men and women and fear Allāh through Whom you demand your mutual (rights), and (do not cut the relations of) the wombs (kinship). Surely, Allāh is Ever an All-Watcher over you." [Sūrah an-Nisāʾ (4):1]

Allāh said:

﴿ يَٰٓأَيُّهَا ٱلَّذِينَ ءَامَنُواْ ٱتَّقُواْ ٱللَّهَ وَقُولُواْ قَوۡلٗا سَدِيدٗا ٧٠ يُصۡلِحۡ لَكُمۡ أَعۡمَٰلَكُمۡ وَيَغۡفِرۡ لَكُمۡ ذُنُوبَكُمۡۗ وَمَن يُطِعِ ٱللَّهَ وَرَسُولَهُۥ فَقَدۡ فَازَ فَوۡزًا عَظِيمًا ٧١ ﴾

"O you who believe! Keep your duty to Allāh and fear Him, and speak (always) the truth. He will direct you to do righteous good deeds and will forgive you your sins. And whosoever obeys Allāh and His Messenger (ﷺ) he has indeed achieved a great achievement (i.e., he will be saved from the Hellfire and made to enter Paradise)." [Sūrah al-ʾAḥzāb (33):70-71]

To proceed:

The most truthful speech is the book of Allāh, and the best of guidance is that of Muḥammad (صَلَّى ٱللَّٰهُ عَلَيْهِ وَسَلَّمَ). The worst evils are religious innovation, and every religious innovation is misguidance, and every misguidance leads to Hellfire.

To proceed:

The fourth pillar of Islām is fasting. It is one of Allāh's obligations and an unequivocal institution in Islām, proven by the Qur'ān and Sunnah.*[1]

[1] This lecture is taken from the explanation of a book called: "Al-Jawhara al-Farīda"; chapter: an overview of the pillars of Islām: Zakat. This lecture was given on Tuesday, 24th of Dhul Hijja 1437; 9/6/2016.

A BRIEF ACCOUNT ON THE VIRTUES OF FASTING

Each act of worship one devotes to Allāh Almighty is tied with several virtues. Whether it is prayer, Zakat, Hajj, or Fasting, all of them are laden with numerous virtues. Plainly clear verses are expressed in the Noble Book of Allāh, encouraging [Muslims] to fast to draw oneself closer to Allāh Almighty. Also, these verses explore the virtues of fasting. Consider the saying of Allāh (سُبْحَانَهُۥ وَتَعَالَىٰ):

﴿ إِنَّ ٱلْمُسْلِمِينَ وَٱلْمُسْلِمَٰتِ وَٱلْمُؤْمِنِينَ وَٱلْمُؤْمِنَٰتِ
وَٱلْقَٰنِتِينَ وَٱلْقَٰنِتَٰتِ وَٱلصَّٰدِقِينَ وَٱلصَّٰدِقَٰتِ وَٱلصَّٰبِرِينَ وَٱلصَّٰبِرَٰتِ
وَٱلْخَٰشِعِينَ وَٱلْخَٰشِعَٰتِ وَٱلْمُتَصَدِّقِينَ وَٱلْمُتَصَدِّقَٰتِ
وَٱلصَّٰٓئِمِينَ وَٱلصَّٰٓئِمَٰتِ وَٱلْحَٰفِظِينَ فُرُوجَهُمْ وَٱلْحَٰفِظَٰتِ
وَٱلذَّٰكِرِينَ ٱللَّهَ كَثِيرًا وَٱلذَّٰكِرَٰتِ أَعَدَّ ٱللَّهُ لَهُم
مَّغْفِرَةً وَأَجْرًا عَظِيمًا ﴿٣٥﴾ ﴾

"Verily, the Muslims (those who submit to Allāh in Islām) men and women, the believers men and women (who believe in Islāmic Monotheism), the men and the women who are obedient (to Allāh), the men and women who are truthful (in their speech and deeds), the men and the women who are patient (in performing all the duties which Allāh has ordered and in abstaining from all that Allāh

has forbidden), the men and the women who are humble (before their Lord Allāh), the men and the women who give *Sadaqat* (i.e. *Zakat*, and alms, etc.), the men and the women who observe *Ṣawm* (fast) (the obligatory fasting during the month of Ramaḍān, and the optional *Nawafil* fasting), the men and the women who guard their chastity (from illegal sexual acts) and the men and the women who remember Allāh much with their hearts and tongues (while sitting, standing, lying, etc. for more than 300 times extra over the remembrance of Allāh during the five compulsory congregational prayers) or praying extra additional *Nawafil* prayers of night in the last part of night, etc.) Allāh has prepared for them forgiveness and a great reward (i.e., Paradise).” [Sūrah al-ʾAḥzāb (33):35]

Allāh (تَبَارَكَ وَتَعَالَىٰ) extended such a great reward and forgiveness to fasting men and women. Allāh (سُبْحَانَهُ وَتَعَالَىٰ) also said:

﴿ وَأَن تَصُومُوا۟ خَيْرٌ لَّكُمْ إِن كُنتُمْ تَعْلَمُونَ ١٨٤ ﴾

“And that you fast, it is better for you if only you know.” [Sūrah al-Baqarah (2):184]

As the reliable traditions of the Sunnah inform us, the Messenger (صَلَّى ٱللَّهُ عَلَيْهِ وَسَلَّمَ) made it clear that fasting is a sturdy block against lusts and imparts protection against Hellfire, simply because Allāh Almighty privileged fasting men and women with a particular gate to Paradise.

Furthermore, fasting weans the soul off thirsting after lusts and disrupts its habits to develop inner peace. In search of proofs, sound Prophetic Ḥadīth so plainly expound on the great reward of fasting.

Consider this one, “**Fasting is a shield**.” It is very similar to the shield worn by a fighter to protect him against the assaults of the enemies. In a command to the individual failing to suppress his lust though incapable of Marriage, the Prophet (صَلَّى ٱللَّهُ عَلَيْهِ وَسَلَّمَ) ordered him to fast in hopes of restraining such desire. Pondering on the Prophet’s words, he resembled fasting to a *Wijā’* (i.e., to castrate the testicles of the male animal with two rocks to cut off the source of lust). Similarly, fasting seals off desire, as explained by the Messenger (peace and blessings be upon him), because it restrains the powers of one’s limbs, puts them at ease, and prevents them from acting uncontrollably.

Granted, fasting is proven to induce an extraordinary impact on the body, internally and externally. Due to the above reasons, both al-Bukhārī and Muslim recorded a sound ḥadīth on the authority of ʿAlqama from ibn Masʿūd who reported that the Prophet (صَلَّى ٱللَّهُ عَلَيْهِ وَسَلَّمَ) said:

يَا مَعْشَرَ ٱلشَّبَابِ ! مَنِ اسْتَطَاعَ مِنْكُمُ ٱلْبَاءَةَ فَلْيَتَزَوَّجْ , فَإِنَّهُ أَغَضُّ لِلْبَصَرِ , وَأَحْصَنُ لِلْفَرْجِ , وَمَنْ لَمْ يَسْتَطِعْ فَعَلَيْهِ بِالصَّوْمِ ; فَإِنَّهُ لَهُ وِجَاءٌ.

> **“Young men, whoever among you can afford it, let him get married, for it keeps you from [unlawful] gazing and preserves you from immorality, but those who cannot devote themselves to fasting, for it is a means of suppressing sexual desire.”**[2]

Affording Marriage here refers to the [financial and physical] capabilities of Marriage.

---

[2] Recorded by al-Bukhārī in his Ṣaḥīḥ collection: (4/119) no. (1905) and Muslim: (2/1018, 1019) no. (1400).

Reflect on how the Prophet (ﷺ) balanced out between Marriage on one side and fasting on the other side.

يَا مَعْشَرَ ٱلشَّبَابِ ! مَنِ اسْتَطَاعَ مِنْكُمُ ٱلْبَاءَةَ فَلْيَتَزَوَّجْ , فَإِنَّهُ أَغَضُّ لِلْبَصَرِ , وَأَحْصَنُ لِلْفَرْجِ , وَمَنْ لَمْ يَسْتَطِعْ ...

"Young men, whoever among you can afford it, let him get married, for it keeps you from [unlawful] gazing and preserves you from immorality, but those who cannot,"

What is their alternative? He (ﷺ) answered:

فَعَلَيْهِ بِالصَّوْمِ ; فَإِنَّهُ لَهُ وِجَاءٌ".

"should devote themselves to fasting, for it is a means of suppressing sexual desire."

The Prophet (ﷺ) clearly expressed that:

أَنَّ الْـجَنَّةَ مَـحْفُوفَـةٌ بِالْـمَكَارِهِ، وَأَنَّ النَّارَ قَدْ حُفَّتْ بِالشَّهَوَاتِ.

"paradise is enclaved with hardships while the hellfire is enclaved with temptations." [3]

Given that fasting suppresses sexual desires that, by nature, lead to Hellfire, the conclusion is that fasting stands between the fasting individual and Hellfire. For this reason, many Ḥadīth unequivocally prove that fasting is a shield against Hellfire.

In the agreed-upon ḥadīth, the Prophet (ﷺ) said:

---

[3] Recorded by al-Bukhārī in his Ṣaḥīḥ collection: (11/320) no. (6487) and Muslim: (4/2174) no. (2823). It is reported on the authority of abū Huraira.

مَا مِنْ عَبْدٍ يَصُومُ يَوْمًا فِي سَبِيلِ اللهِ إِلَّا بَاعَدَ اللهُ بِذَلِكَ الْيَوْمِ وَجْهَهُ عَنِ النَّارِ سَبْعِينَ خَرِيفًا.

"Any servant of Allāh who fasts for a day in the Cause of Allāh, Allāh will keep his face from Hellfire at a distance of seventy years." [4]

It means that the distance keeping the individual afar from Hellfire equals a seventy-year walking distance.

The Prophet (ﷺ) said:

الصِّيَامُ جُنَّةٌ يَسْتَجِنُّ بِهَا الْعَبْدُ مِنَ النَّارِ.

"Fasting is a shield protecting the individual from hellfire." [5]

It safeguards the individual against the brushes of Fire. Imām Ahmad recorded this ḥadīth on the authority of Jābir.

The Prophet (ﷺ) said:

---

[4] Recorded by al-Bukhārī in his Ṣaḥīḥ collection: (6/47) no. (2840) and Muslim: (2/808) no. (1153). The above wording is that of Muslim on the authority of abū Saʿīd al-Khudrī (may Allāh be pleased with him).

[5] Recorded by Ahmad in 'Al-Musnad': (3/341, 396) and al-Bayhaqī in 'Shu`ab al-'Īmān): (5/193, 203) no. (3292, 3308). It is reported on the authority of Jābir (may Allāh be pleased with him).

Al-Albānī graded this ḥadīth as *ṣaḥīḥ li-Ghayrihī* (sound for extraneous reasons) in his book ʾṢaḥīḥ al-Targhīb wa al-Tarhīb': (1/578) no. (981). Other versions of this ḥadīth are reported by ʿUthmān ibn abū al-ʿĀṣ al-Thaqafī, ʿĀʾisha, abū Huraira, Anas, and Bishr ibn al-Khaṣāṣiyya. A part of this ḥadīth is reported in both Ṣaḥīḥ collections on the authority of abū Huraira.

مَنْ صَامَ يَوْمًا فِي سَبِيلِ اللهِ جَعَلَ اللهُ بَيْنَهُ وَبَيْنَ النَّارِ خَنْدَقًا كَمَا بَيْنَ السَّمَاءِ وَالْأَرْضِ.

"Any servant of Allāh who fasts for a day in the Cause of Allāh, Allāh will keep him afar from Hell-fire at a distance equivalent to that between heaven and the earth." [6]

This ḥadīth is recorded by Imām al-Tirmidhī and was graded as ḥasan (sound).

"Some Ḥadīth scholars deemed the reports above on the virtue of fasting as restricted to Fasting during Jihad for the sake of Allāh. However, fasting at any day with a sincere intention for the sake of Allāh Almighty and in accordance with the manner prescribed by the Messenger (peace and blessings be upon him) is categorized as fasting in the Cause of Allāh." [7]

The fighter in Jihād needs his full strength to defend the religion of his Lord. Therefore, it is very strange to limit the previous reports to Jihād. Fasting sincerely for the sake of Allāh, the Lord of the worlds, even if it is just a single day, Allāh Almighty keeps the face of this individual afar from Hellfire at a seventy-year walking distance.

Fasting is a means to Paradise because it distances the individual away from Hellfire, only to draw him closer to

---

[6] Al-Tirmidhī recorded this ḥadīth in ʾal-Jāmiʿ: (4/167) no. (1624). He graded it as ḥasan gharīb (good but reported from an uncommon chain of transmission). Al-Albānī graded this ḥadīth as ḥasan (good) in his book al-*Ṣaḥīḥa*: (2/106) no. (563). He added, "This ḥadīth has a parallel version that supports it reported on the authority of Abū al-Dardāʾ who elevated it to the Prophet."

[7] Al-Targhīb wa al-Tarhīb' by al-Mundhrī and edited by al-Albānī (1/581).

heaven until he is situated squarely at the heart of Paradise, enjoying the best of everything.[8]

Abū `Umāma (رَضِيَٱللَّهُعَنْهُ) reported, "I asked the Messenger of Allāh to guide me to deed that admits me to paradise. He told me:

عَلَيْكَ بِالصَّوْمِ، لَا مِثْلَ لَـهُ

"Adhere to fasting because it is unparalleled."[9]

This Ḥadīth is Ṣaḥīḥ. It is recorded by al-Nasā`ī and graded as Ṣaḥīḥ al-Albānī. The Prophet (صَلَّىٱللَّهُعَلَيْهِوَسَلَّمَ) guided him to a single deed that guarantees admission to Paradise. Such is a major good deed and beloved to Allāh (تَبَارَكَوَتَعَالَىٰ). His advice, "**Adhere to fasting because it is unparalleled,**" indicates that he would have informed him that had there been any better deed.

وَالصَّائِمُونَ يُوَفَّوْنَ أُجُورَهُمْ بِغَيْرِ حِسَابٍ

"Fasting individuals will receive rewards without measure.[10]

لِلصَّائِمِ فَرْحَتَانِ

---

[8] *Sharḥ al-Mishkā* by al-Ṭaybī: (12/3844) no. (6011) and Tuḥfat al-Aḥwadhī by al-Mubārakfūrī: (6/321).

[9] Recorded by al-Nasā`ī in 'al-Mujtabā: (4/165) no. (2222, 2223). In another version, it reads, "…noting equals fasting." The ḥadīth is graded as Ṣaḥīḥ by al-Albānī in Ṣaḥīḥ al-Targhīb wa al-Tarhīb': (1/580) no. (986).

[10] In his book 'al-Jāmi`: (192, 193) no. (318), ibn Wahb recorded a ḥadīth with a fair chain of transmission on the authority of Ka`b who said, "**On the Day of Judgment, a caller will make an announcement: Every cultivator shall not only be rewarded in correspondence with his deeds but even extra. Only the people invested in the Qur`ān and fasting shall be rewarded without measure.**"

"The fasting individual sees happiness in two occasions."[11]

وَخَلُوفُ فَمِ الصَّائِـمِ أَطْيَبُ عِنْدَ اللهِ مِنْ رِيحِ الْمِسْكِ

"Allāh considers the smell of the fasting person's mouth better than that of musk."[12]

"The smell of the fasting person's mouth" refers to the unpleasant smell emanating from the mouth as a natural result of refraining from food and drink. As recorded by al-Bukhārī and Muslim, Abū Hurayrah (رَضِيَٱللَّهُعَنْهُ) reported that the Messenger of Allāh (صَلَّىٱللَّهُعَلَيْهِوَسَلَّمَ) said:

كُلُّ عَمَلِ ابْنِ آدَمَ لَـهُ إِلَّا الصِّيَامَ

"Every good deed is for the individual except for fasting."[13]

It means each good deed one does is promised a particularly limited reward (but indeed, Allāh's benevolence is extraordinary). Fasting, on the other hand, is rewarded without measure.

In an alternative interpretation, superficial deeds have a clear and visible end, whereas fasting is built on two principles: an intention and refrainment from food, drink, and lust. In a way, refrainment is

---

[11] Recorded by al-Bukhārī in his Ṣaḥīḥ collection: (4/118) no. (1904) and Muslim: (2/806) no. (1151) on the authority of Abū Huraira who reported that the Messenger of Allāh (peace and blessings be upon him), "**By the One in whose hand is the soul of Muḥammad, the smell coming from the mouth of the fasting person is better before Allāh than the fragrance of musk. The fasting person has two moments of joy: When he breaks his fasting he rejoices at breaking his fast and when he meets his Lord, the Mighty and Sublime, he will rejoice for fasting.**" In the version recorded by Muslim, "….and when he meets Allāh, Allāh will reward him with happiness."

[12] Reference previously mentioned.

[13] Cited earlier.

something negative, therefore tying the whole issue of fasting with the intention. Scholars argued that if a person begins his day intending to fast, continued throughout the day without breaking his fast until close to sunset, at which he intended to break his fast yet without consuming anything to nullify the fasting such as eating, drinking, or engaging a sexual desire, this person is considered to have broken his fasting, simply because the intention is an essential principle.

Even though such a person refrained from consuming any food, drink, or lust, he violated the principle of intention, an invisible deed whose knowledge is only accessible to Allāh (تَبَارَكَ وَتَعَالَى). The majority of other acts are visible and have their respective effects going beyond the individual. When fasting, however, none is watching the individual except Allāh. One can go to hiding anywhere and breaks his fasting, but only Allāh can see him.

يَقُولُ اللهُ (جَلَّ وَعَلَا): كُلُّ عَمَلِ ابْنِ آدَمَ لَهُ إِلَّا الصِّيَامَ؛ فَإِنَّهُ لِي وَأَنَا أَجْزِي بِهِ، وَالصِّيَامُ جُنَّةٌ، وَإِذَا كَانَ يَوْمُ صَوْمِ أَحَدِكُمْ فَلَا يَرْفُثْ وَلَا يَصْخَبْ، فَإِنْ سَابَّهُ أَحَدٌ أَوْ قَاتَلَهُ فَلْيَقُلْ: إِنِّي امْرُؤٌ صَائِمٌ.

"Allāh Almighty said, 'Every act of the son of Adam is for him, except fasting, which is (exclusively) for Me, and I will reward him for it.' Fasting is a shield. When anyone of you is observing fast, he should neither indulge in obscene language nor should he raise his voice, and if anyone reviles him or tries to quarrel with him, he should say: 'I am fasting."[14]

[14] Cited earlier.

"...**he should say: 'I am fasting**." It means to speak this phrase up and make it audible to the abuser to stop the abuser and the quarreler. Other scholars suggested that this statement is intended to restrain oneself from exchanging insults and quarreling in the way of self-reminding.

As one version reads, **'I am fasting, I am fasting,'** it reminds oneself of fasting and reminding the insulter or the quarreler to stop. However, the first opinion is more likely, namely to speak it out. Generally, when the word **'say'** is instructed, it refers to audible utterance.

وَالَّذِي نَفْسُ مُـحَمَّدٍ بِيَدِهِ لَـخُلُوفُ فَـمِ الصَّائِـمِ أَطْيَـبُ عِنْدَ اللهِ مِنْ رِيحِ الْمِسْكِ لِلـصَّائِـمِ فَرْحَتَانِ يَفْرَحُهُمَا: إِذَا أَفْطَرَ فَرِحَ، وَإِذَا لَقِيَ رَبَّـهُ فَرِحَ بِصَوْمِـهِ.

"By the One in whose hand is the soul of Muḥammad, the smell coming from the mouth of the fasting person is better before Allāh than the fragrance of musk. The fasting person has two moments of joy: When he breaks his fasting, he rejoices at breaking his fast, and when one meets his Lord, the Mighty and Sublime, he will rejoice for fasting."

In another version by al-Bukhārī,

يَتْـرُكُ طَعَامَـهُ وَشَـرَابَـهُ وَشَـهْوَتَـهُ مِنْ أَجْلِـي، الصِّيَامُ لِي وَأَنَا أَجْزِي بِهِ، وَالْـحَسَنَةُ بِـعَشْـرِ أَمْثَالِـهَا.

"[the fasting person] abstains his food, drink, and lust for My sake. The [reward] of fasting belongs to Me, and each good deed has ten times each reward."[15]

In a narration by Muslim,

كُـلُّ عَمَلِ ابْنِ آدَمَ يُضَاعَفُ، الْـحَسَنَةُ عَشْرُ أَمْثَالِهَا إِلَى سَبْعِمَائَـةِ ضِعْفٍ، قَالَ اللهُ تَعَالَى: إِلَّا الصَّوْمَ فَإِنَّـهُ لِي، وَأَنَا أَجْزِي بِـهِ، يَدَعُ شَهْـوَتَـهُ وَطَعَامَـهُ لِأَجْلِي، وَلِلصَّائِـمِ فَرْحَتَانِ: فَرْحَةٌ عِنْدَ فِطْرِهِ، وَفَرْحَةٌ عِنْدَ لِقَاءِ رَبِّـهِ، وَلَـخُلُوفُ فَمِ الصَّائِـمِ أَطْيَبُ عِنْدَ اللهِ مِنْ رِيحِ الْمِسْكِ.

"The reward of every (good) deed of a person is multiplied from ten to seven hundred times. Allāh Almighty says: 'The reward of fasting is different from the reward of other good deeds; fasting is for Me, and I Alone will give its reward. The fasting person abstains from food and drink only for My sake.' The fasting person has two joyous occasions, one at the time of breaking his fast and the other when meeting his Lord. Surely, the breath of the fasting is better smelling to Allāh than the fragrance of musk."[16]

Unlike other good deeds whose reward is multiplied as much as seven hundred times or more, the reward of fasting transcends this limit because Allāh took it upon Himself to reward it. It is common knowledge that the enforcer's power determines the extent of an impact. The power of Allāh, the Lord of the worlds, is limitless, and His generosity knows no boundaries.

---

[15] Recorded by al-Bukhārī: (4/102) no. (1894).
[16] Recorded by Muslim: (2/708) no. (1151).

Fasting and [recitation] of the Qur'ān intercede for the individual:

The Prophet (ﷺ) said:

الصِّيَامُ وَالْقُرْآنُ يَشْفَعَانِ لِلْعَبْدِ يَوْمَ الْقِيَامَةِ، يَقُولُ الصِّيَامُ: أَيْ رَبِّ! مَنَعْتُهُ الطَّعَامَ وَالشَّهْوَةَ؛ فَشَفِّعْنِي فِيهِ، وَيَقُولُ الْقُرْآنُ: مَنَعْتُهُ النَّوْمَ بِاللَّيْلِ؛ فَشَفِّعْنِي فِيهِ، قَالَ: فَيُشَفَّعَانِ.

> **"Fasting and the Qur'ān intercede for a man. Fasting says, 'O my Lord, I have kept him away from his food and his lusts by day, so accept my intercession for him.' The Qur'ān says, 'I have kept him away from sleep by night, so accept my intercession for him.' Then their intercession is accepted."**[17]

This ḥadīth's grade is good, and it is reported on the authority of 'Abdullāh ibn 'Amr (رَضِيَ اللَّهُ عَنْهُمَا) from the Prophet (ﷺ). Imām Ahmad and al-Ḥākim in 'al-Mustadrak' record it.

Fasting brings the expiation of sins:

Allāh (تَبَارَكَ وَتَعَالَى) privileged fasting with virtues unfound in the remaining acts of worship. To name one, it is a means to amend shaving the head during the state of *Ihram* due to an illness or sustaining an injury in the head. Allāh Almighty made fasting the

---

[17] Recorded by ibn al-Mubārak in 'al-Zuhd' on the authority of Nu'aym ibn Ḥammād: (16/517) no. (385); Ahmad in 'al-Musnad': (2/174) no. (6626); al-Mirwazī in 'Mukhtaṣar Qiyām al-Layl': (46); al-Ṭabarānī in 'al-Mu'jam al-Kabīr': (13/38) no. (88); and al-Ḥākim in 'al-Mustadrak': (1/554) no. (2036). This ḥadīth is reported on the authority of 'Abdullah ibn 'Amr (may Allāh be pleased with him and his father). Al-Ḥākim commented, "This ḥadīth is sound." Al-Albānī graded it as good in 'Tamām al-Minna': (394, 395).

way to amend this issue. Fasting is interestingly a means to amend several actions such as the incapability of offering sacrifice (in Ḥajj), killing inadvertently a non-Muslim who is promised safety, violation of self-taken oath, killing a game during Ihram, and *Ẓihār* (saying to one's wife: you are like my mother's back as a way of giving up sexual intercourse). These instances are highlighted in the Book of Allāh (تَبَارَكَ وَتَعَالَى), which reflects the excellence of this act of worship.

In the instance of shaving the head during Ihram due to an illness, Allāh (جَلَّ جَلَالُهُ) said:

﴿ وَأَتِمُّوا۟ ٱلْحَجَّ وَٱلْعُمْرَةَ لِلَّهِ ۚ فَإِنْ أُحْصِرْتُمْ فَمَا ٱسْتَيْسَرَ مِنَ ٱلْهَدْىِ ۖ وَلَا تَحْلِقُوا۟ رُءُوسَكُمْ حَتَّىٰ يَبْلُغَ ٱلْهَدْىُ مَحِلَّهُۥ ۚ فَمَن كَانَ مِنكُم مَّرِيضًا أَوْ بِهِۦٓ أَذًى مِّن رَّأْسِهِۦ فَفِدْيَةٌ مِّن صِيَامٍ أَوْ صَدَقَةٍ أَوْ نُسُكٍ ۚ ﴾

"And perform properly (i.e., all the ceremonies according to the ways of Prophet Muḥammad صَلَّى ٱللَّهُ عَلَيْهِ وَسَلَّمَ), the *Ḥajj* and '*Umrah* (i.e., the pilgrimage to Makkah) for Allāh. But if you are prevented (from completing them), sacrifice a *Hady* (animal, i.e., a sheep, a cow, or a camel, etc.) such as you can afford and do not shave your heads until the *Hady* reaches the place of sacrifice. And whosoever of you is ill or has an ailment in his scalp (necessitating shaving), he must pay a *Fidyah* (ransom) of either observing *Ṣawm* (fasts) (three days) or giving *Sadaqah* (charity – feeding six poor persons) or offering sacrifice (one sheep)." [Sūrah al-Baqarah (2):196]

Hence, ransoming is performed by fasting, charity, or offering a sacrifice. Then Allāh (تَبَارَكَ وَتَعَالَىٰ) said afterward:

﴿فَإِذَآ أَمِنتُمۡ فَمَن تَمَتَّعَ بِٱلۡعُمۡرَةِ إِلَى ٱلۡحَجِّ فَمَا ٱسۡتَيۡسَرَ مِنَ ٱلۡهَدۡيِۚ
فَمَن لَّمۡ يَجِدۡ فَصِيَامُ ثَلَٰثَةِ أَيَّامٖ فِي ٱلۡحَجِّ وَسَبۡعَةٍ إِذَا رَجَعۡتُمۡۗ تِلۡكَ
عَشَرَةٞ كَامِلَةٞۗ ذَٰلِكَ لِمَن لَّمۡ يَكُنۡ أَهۡلُهُۥ حَاضِرِي ٱلۡمَسۡجِدِ ٱلۡحَرَامِۚ وَٱتَّقُواْ
ٱللَّهَ وَٱعۡلَمُوٓاْ أَنَّ ٱللَّهَ شَدِيدُ ٱلۡعِقَابِ ١٩٦﴾

"Then if you are in safety and whosoever performs the *'Umrah* in the months of *Ḥajj,* before (performing) the *Ḥajj,* (i.e., *Hajj-at-Tamattu'* and *Al-Qiran*), he must slaughter a *Hady* such as he can afford, but if one cannot afford it, he should observe *Ṣawm* (fasts) three days during the *Ḥajj* and seven days after his return (to his home), making ten days in all. This is for him whose family is not present at *Al-Masjid-al-Haram* (i.e., a non-resident of Makkah). And fear Allāh much and know that Allāh is Severe in punishment." [Sūrah al-Baqarah (2):196]

In the instance of killing inadvertently a non-Muslim who is promised safety, Allāh (جَلَّ جَلَالُهُ) said:

﴿وَإِن كَانَ مِن قَوۡمِۭ بَيۡنَكُمۡ وَبَيۡنَهُم مِّيثَٰقٞ فَدِيَةٞ مُّسَلَّمَةٌ
إِلَىٰٓ أَهۡلِهِۦ وَتَحۡرِيرُ رَقَبَةٖ مُّؤۡمِنَةٖۖ فَمَن لَّمۡ يَجِدۡ فَصِيَامُ

شَهْرَيْنِ مُتَتَابِعَيْنِ تَوْبَةً مِّنَ ٱللَّهِ ۗ وَكَانَ ٱللَّهُ عَلِيمًا
حَكِيمًا ﴿٩٢﴾

"and if he belonged to a people with whom you have a treaty of mutual alliance, compensation (blood money – *Diya*) must be paid to his family, and a believing slave must be freed. And whoso finds this (the penance of freeing a slave) beyond his means, he must fast for two consecutive months to seek repentance from Allāh. And Allāh is Ever All-Knowing, All-Wise." [Sūrah an-Nisā' (4):92]

In the instance of violating a self-taken oath, Allāh (جَلَّجَلَالُهُ) said:

﴿ لَا يُؤَاخِذُكُمُ ٱللَّهُ بِٱللَّغْوِ فِيٓ أَيْمَٰنِكُمْ وَلَٰكِن يُؤَاخِذُكُم بِمَا
عَقَّدتُّمُ ٱلْأَيْمَٰنَ ۖ فَكَفَّٰرَتُهُۥٓ إِطْعَامُ عَشَرَةِ مَسَٰكِينَ مِنْ أَوْسَطِ مَا
تُطْعِمُونَ أَهْلِيكُمْ أَوْ كِسْوَتُهُمْ أَوْ تَحْرِيرُ رَقَبَةٍ ۖ فَمَن لَّمْ يَجِدْ
فَصِيَامُ ثَلَٰثَةِ أَيَّامٍ ۚ ذَٰلِكَ كَفَّٰرَةُ أَيْمَٰنِكُمْ إِذَا حَلَفْتُمْ ۚ وَٱحْفَظُوٓا۟
أَيْمَٰنَكُمْ ۚ كَذَٰلِكَ يُبَيِّنُ ٱللَّهُ لَكُمْ ءَايَٰتِهِۦ لَعَلَّكُمْ تَشْكُرُونَ ﴿٨٩﴾

"Allāh will not punish you for what is unintentional in your oaths, but He will punish you for your deliberate oaths; for its expiation (a deliberate oath) feed ten *Masakin* (poor persons), on a scale of the average of that with which you feed your own families; or clothe them; or manumit a slave. But whosoever cannot afford (that), then he should fast for three days. That is the

expiation for the oaths when you have sworn. And protect your oaths (i.e., do not swear much). Thus, Allāh clarifies to you His Ayat (proofs, evidence, verses, lessons, signs, revelations, etc.) that you may be grateful. " [Sūrah al-Mā'idah (5):89]

In the instance of killing a game during Ihrām, Allāh (تَبَارَكَ وَتَعَالَى) said:

﴿ يَٰٓأَيُّهَا ٱلَّذِينَ ءَامَنُواْ لَا تَقۡتُلُواْ ٱلصَّيۡدَ وَأَنتُمۡ حُرُمٞۚ وَمَن قَتَلَهُۥ مِنكُم مُّتَعَمِّدٗا فَجَزَآءٞ مِّثۡلُ مَا قَتَلَ مِنَ ٱلنَّعَمِ يَحۡكُمُ بِهِۦ ذَوَا عَدۡلٖ مِّنكُمۡ هَدۡيَۢا بَٰلِغَ ٱلۡكَعۡبَةِ أَوۡ كَفَّٰرَةٞ طَعَامُ مَسَٰكِينَ أَوۡ عَدۡلُ ذَٰلِكَ صِيَامٗا ﴾

"O you who believe! Kill not game while you are in a state of *Ihram* for *Hajj* or '*Umrah* (pilgrimage), and whosoever of you kills it intentionally, the penalty is an offering, brought to the Ka'bah, of an eatable animal (i.e., sheep, goat, cow, etc.) equivalent to the one he killed, as adjudged by two just men among you; or, for expiation, he should feed *Masakin* (poor persons), or its equivalent in *Saum* (fasting), that he may taste the heaviness (punishment) of his deed. Allāh has forgiven what is past, but Allāh will take retribution from him if he commits it again. And Allāh is All-Mighty, All-Able of Retribution." [Sūrah al-Mā'idah (5):95]

In the instance of *Ẓihār*, Allāh (سُبْحَانَهُ وَتَعَالَى) said:

﴿ وَٱلَّذِينَ يُظَٰهِرُونَ مِن نِّسَآئِهِمْ ثُمَّ يَعُودُونَ لِمَا قَالُوا۟ فَتَحْرِيرُ
رَقَبَةٍ مِّن قَبْلِ أَن يَتَمَآسَّا ۚ ذَٰلِكُمْ تُوعَظُونَ بِهِۦ ۚ وَٱللَّهُ بِمَا تَعْمَلُونَ
خَبِيرٌ ۝٣ فَمَن لَّمْ يَجِدْ فَصِيَامُ شَهْرَيْنِ مُتَتَابِعَيْنِ مِن قَبْلِ أَن
يَتَمَآسَّا ۖ فَمَن لَّمْ يَسْتَطِعْ فَإِطْعَامُ سِتِّينَ مِسْكِينًا ۚ ذَٰلِكَ لِتُؤْمِنُوا۟ بِٱللَّهِ
وَرَسُولِهِۦ ۚ وَتِلْكَ حُدُودُ ٱللَّهِ ۗ وَلِلْكَٰفِرِينَ عَذَابٌ أَلِيمٌ ۝٤ ﴾

"And those who make unlawful to them (their wives) (by *Az-Zihar*) and wish to free themselves from what they uttered, (the penalty) in that case (is) the freeing of a slave before they touch each other. That is an admonition to you (so that you may not return to such an ill thing). And Allāh is All-Aware of what you do. He who finds not (the money for freeing a slave) must fast two successive months before they both touch each other. For him who is unable to do so, he should feed sixty of *Miskin* (poor). That is so that you may have perfect Faith in Allāh and His Messenger. These are the limits set by Allāh. And for disbelievers, there is a painful torment." [Sūrah al-Mujādilah (58):3-4]

In all the above instances, fasting is designated as a means to amend for such wrongdoings. Furthermore, fasting takes part in expiating transgressions committed against one's wealth, family, and neighbor. In the two Ṣaḥīḥ collections, Ḥudhayfah (رَضِيَ ٱللَّهُ عَنْهُ) reported that the Messenger of Allāh (صَلَّى ٱللَّهُ عَلَيْهِ وَسَلَّمَ) said:

فِتْنَةُ الرَّجُلِ فِي أَهْلِهِ وَمالِهِ وَوَلَدِهِ وَجَارِهِ، يُكَفِّرُهَا الصِّيَامُ وَالصَّلَاةُ وَالصَّدَقَةُ وَالْأَمْرُ بِالْمَعْرُوفِ وَالنَّهْيُ عَنِ الْمُنْكَرِ.

"Any wrongdoing one commits against one's family, wealth, children, or neighbor is expiated through fasting, observing prayer, giving out charity, or commanding the good and forbidding the evil."[18]

Allāh, the Lord and Master of all that exists, has privileged the observers of fasting with a particular gate in Paradise accessible only by them but none else. Sahl ibn Sa`d (رَضِيَ ٱللَّهُ عَنْهُ) reported that the Prophet (صَلَّى ٱللَّهُ عَلَيْهِ وَسَلَّمَ) said:

إِنَّ فِي الْجَنَّةِ بَابًا يُقَالُ لَهُ: الرَّيَّانُ.

"There is a special gate in paradise called al-Rayyān (i.e., well-watered)."[19]

Reflect deeply on the compensation dedicated to the observers of fasting who spend their day thirsting. They are rewarded with admission to Paradise through the gate of al-Rayyān (i.e., well-watered). The name of the gate is in remarkable conformity with the reality of fasting.

---

[18] Recorded by al-Bukhārī in his Ṣaḥīḥ collection: (2/8) no. (525) and Muslim: (4/2218) no. (144). In Muslim's version, there is the addition of, "…against wealth, or self…".

[19] Recorded by al-Bukhārī in his Ṣaḥīḥ collection: (4/111) no. (1896) and Muslim: (2/808) no. (1152).

يَدْخُلُ مِنْهُ الصَّائِمُونَ يَوْمَ الْقِيَامَـةِ، لَا يَدْخُلُ مِنْهُ أَحَدٌ غَيْـرُهُمْ، فَإِذَا دَخَلُوا أُغْلِـقَ.

"The observers of fasting will enter through this gate on the Day of Judgment. None else will enter through this gate. Once all of them finish entering, it is closed."

Observers of Fasting refer to individuals who developed the habit of fasting to become their most-observed act of worship. On the Day of Judgment, Allāh Almighty rewards them by entering Paradise through the gate of **al-Rayyān**. Only those who fast abundantly shall enter through that gate.

More attractively, if one is habitually absorbed in another pious act besides fasting, the compensation is an offer of access to enter Paradise through any of the eight gates, as the Prophet (صَلَّى ٱللَّهُ عَلَيْهِ وَسَلَّمَ), promised Abū Bakr that:

أَنَّـهُ يُدْعَى مِنْ جَمِيعِ أَبْوَابِ الْـجَنَّـةِ

"He shall be invited from all the gates of paradise."[20]

[20] Recorded by al-Bukhārī in his Ṣaḥīḥ collection: (4/111) no. (1897) and Muslim: (2/711, 712) no. (1027). Abū Huraira (may Allāh be pleased with him) reported that the Messenger of Allāh (peace and blessings be upon him) said, "**Whoever gives two kinds (of things or property) in charity for Allāh's Cause will be called from the gates of Paradise and will be addressed, 'O servant of Allāh! Here is prosperity.' So, whoever was amongst the people who were used to offer their prayers will be called from the gate of the prayer; and whoever was amongst the people who were used to participate in Jihad will be called from the gate of Jihad; and whoever was amongst those who were used to observe fasting will be called from the gate of al-Rayyān; whoever was amongst those who were used to give in charity will be called from the gate of charity**." Abu Bakr said, "Let my parents be sacrificed for you, O Allāh's Messenger (peace and blessings be upon him)! No distress or need will befall him

He earned such a grand reward because he moderated balance in all of the good deeds he observed, not to mention his performance to perfection (رَضِيَٱللَّهُعَنْهُ).

فَإِذَا دَخَلُوا أُغْلِقَ، فَلَـمْ يَدْخُلْ مِنْـهُ أَحَدٌ

"Once they finish entering, none else will enter."

Al-Nasāʿī's version contains an addition that reads,

فَإِذَا دَخَلَ آخِرُهُمْ أُغْلِقَ، وَمَنْ دَخَلَ شَرِبَ، وَمَنْ شَرِبَ لَـمْ يَظْـمَأْ أَبَدًا.

"Once the last of them enters, the gate is closed. Whoever is inside will drink, and whoever drinks will never feel thirst ever again."[21]

This was a summary of the general virtues of fasting.*[22]

Turning to fasting in Ramaḍān in particular:

---

who will be called from those gates. Will there be any one who will be called from all these gates?" The Prophet (peace and blessings be upon him) replied, "**Yes, and I hope you will be one of them.**"

In another narration recorded by al-Bukhārī and Muslim, it reads, "**Whoever gives two kinds (of things or property) in charity for Allāh's Cause, the gatekeepers of Paradise will call him from the gates of Paradise (saying): O So-and-so, come and enter!**'

[21] Recorded by al-Nasāʿī in "al-Mujtabā': (4/168) no. (2236). On the authority of Sahl ibn Sa`d who reported that the Prophet (peace and blessings be upon him) said, "**The observers of fasting are privileged with a gate in paradise called al-Rayyān. No one will enter through it but them. Once the last of them enters, the gate is closed. Whoever is inside will drink, and whoever drinks will never feel thirst ever again.**" This ḥadīth is graded as ḥasan (good) by al-Albānī in 'Ṣaḥīḥ al-Targhīb wa al-Tarhīb': (1/577) no. (979).

[22] This part is taken from a lecture the Shaykh delivered on Sha`ban 4th 1427/ 6/28/2006. It is titled, "The excellence of fasting and the month of Ramaḍān. Introducing some rulings pertaining Ramaḍān."

There are countless Ramaḍān-specific good deeds by which one seeks the pleasure of the Most Compassionate and Most Merciful. However, the greatest one is fasting, as indicated by the Prophet (صَلَّى ٱللَّٰهُ عَلَيْهِ وَسَلَّمَ) who said:

مَنْ صَامَ رَمَضَانَ إِيمَانًا وَاحْتِسَابًا غُفِرَ لَهُ مَا تَقَدَّمَ مِنْ ذَنْبِهِ.

"Whoever fasts Ramaḍān while driven by faith and hope in Allāh's reward, his past sins will be forgiven."[23]

The ḥadīth is recorded in both Ṣaḥīḥ collections. In short, fasting is the grandest good deed in the month of Ramaḍān.*[24]

On the last night of Ramaḍān, Allāh, the Lord of the Worlds, forgives the sins of those who fast:

وَلِلَّهِ جَلَّ وَعَلَا عُتَقَاءُ مِنَ النَّارِ، وَذَلِكَ كُلَّ لَيْلَةٍ مِنْ رَمَضَانَ.

"Allāh frees people from the hellfire every night of Ramaḍān."[25]

The observant of fasting is granted an answered supplication. Anas reported that the Messenger of Allāh (صَلَّى ٱللَّٰهُ عَلَيْهِ وَسَلَّمَ) said:

---

[23] Cited earlier.

[24] This small part is taken from a Friday sermon delivered on Ramaḍān 15th 1433 / 8/3/2012. It is titled, "How to live Ramaḍān?".

[25] Recorded by al-Tirmidhī in 'al-Jāmi`': (3/57) no. (682), ibn Māja in 'al-Sunan': (1/526) no. (1642) on the authority of Abū Huraira (may Allāh be pleased with him). This ḥadīth is graded as ḥasan (good) by al-Albānī in 'Ṣaḥīḥ al-Targhīb wa al-Tarhīb': (1/585) no. (998). It is reported on the authority of abū Sa'īd, ibn 'Umar, ibn 'Abbās, ibn Mas'ūd, Jābir, Abū 'Umāma (may Allāh be pleased with them) and al-Ḥasan in a Mursal form.

ثَلَاثُ دَعَوَاتٍ لَا تُـرَدُّ: دَعْوَةُ الْوَالِـدِ، وَدَعْوَةُ الصَّائِـمِ، وَدَعْوَةُ الْـمُـسَافِـرِ.

"Three individuals will have their supplications answered: the parent, the observant of fasting, and the traveler."[26] *[27]

Fasting is for Allāh, the Lord of the worlds, to reward:

كُـلُّ عَمَلِ ابْنِ آدَمَ لَـهُ إِلَّا الصَّوْمَ فَإِنَّـهُ لِي وَأَنَا أَجْزِي بِـهِ.

"Every good deed the individual does is for him except for fasting; it is for Me, and I reward it."[28]

Fasting is to be observed sincerely for the sake of Allāh. In return, Allāh will reward it abundantly and countlessly, provided that the fasting individual complies with the commands of Allāh and following the guidance of the Messenger of Allāh (صَلَّى ٱللَّهُ عَلَيْهِ وَسَلَّمَ). *[29]

---

[26] Recorded by al-Bayhaqī in 'al-Sunnan al-Kubrā': (3/345) no. (6392), ʿAsākir in 'Muʿjam al-Shuyūkh': (1/338) no. (405), al-Rāfiʿī in Akhbār Qazwīn (3/114), and al-Ḍiyāʾ in al-Mukhtāra (6/74, 75) no. (2057). Al-Albānī graded this ḥadīth as ḥasan (good) based on its various parallel versions in his book 'al- ʾṢaḥīḥa': (4/406), no. (1797). Abū Huraira reported a similar narration.

[27] This small part is taken from a Friday sermon delivered on Ramaḍān 15th 1433 / 8/3/2012. It is titled, "How to live Ramaḍān?".

[28] Recorded by al-Bukhārī in his Ṣaḥīḥ collection: (10/3691) no. (5927) and Muslim: (2/806) no. (1151) on the authority of Abū Huraira who reported that the Messenger of Allāh (peace and blessings be upon him) said, "**Every good deed of the individual does is for him except fasting; it is for Me. and I shall reward (the fasting person) for it.' Verily, the smell of the mouth of a fasting person is better to Allāh than the smell of musk.**"

[29] This part is taken from a Friday sermon delivered on Dhul Hijjah 4th 1436 / 9/18/2015. It is titled "The way for whoever intends to perform Hajj and 'Umrah".

OBJECTIVES AND BENEFITS OF FASTING

Allāh, the Lord of the Worlds, mandated fasting the month of Ramaḍān on Muslims. He embedded fasting with tremendous benefits and privileges. When Ramaḍān is observed appropriately, the individual shall, by Allāh's will, gain the pleasure of Allāh (تَبَارَكَ وَتَعَالَىٰ). *[30]

A fruit of fasting is having Taqwā of Allāh:

Allāh (سُبْحَانَهُ وَتَعَالَىٰ) clearly expressed the wise goal behind the obligation of fasting. Allāh said:

﴿ يَـٰٓأَيُّهَا ٱلَّذِينَ ءَامَنُوا۟ كُتِبَ عَلَيْكُمُ ٱلصِّيَامُ كَمَا كُتِبَ عَلَى ٱلَّذِينَ مِن قَبْلِكُمْ لَعَلَّكُمْ تَتَّقُونَ ﴿١٨٣﴾ ﴾

"O you who believe! Observing *As-Ṣawm* (the fasting) is prescribed for you as it was prescribed for those before you, that you may become *Al-Muttaqun* (the pious – see V.2:2)." [Sūrah al-Baqarah (2):183]

It means: In the same way we mandated fasting on previous nations, We mandated it on the believers perhaps they should develop Taqwā of Allāh through fulfilling this obligation.[31]

---

[30] This part is taken from a lecture delivered on Monday Ramaḍān 1st 1432 / 8/1/2011.

[31] Al-Tafsīr al-Wasīṭ: (1/381).

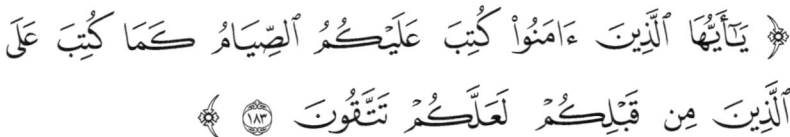

Indeed, to have Taqwā of Allāh is to reach the loftiest of ranks and secure the pleasure of Allāh as well as those who are pleased with Allāh. Allāh (سُبْحَانَهُ وَتَعَالَىٰ) said:

﴿ إِنَّ أَكْرَمَكُمْ عِندَ ٱللَّهِ أَتْقَىٰكُمْ ۚ إِنَّ ٱللَّهَ عَلِيمٌ خَبِيرٌ ﴿١٣﴾ ﴾

"Verily, the most honorable of you with Allāh is that (believer) who has *At-Taqwa* [i.e., one of the *Muttaqun* (pious – see V.2:2)]. Verily, Allāh is All-Knowing, All-Aware." [Sūrah al-Hujuraat (49):13]

Having Taqwā of Allāh is achieved through compliance with the commands and refrainment from prohibitions. Failing to achieve having Taqwā of Allāh through Fasting renders it valueless and vain, just like a bad harvest at the end of the season. It is genuinely unfortunate to farm the land, water and fertilize it, and work tirelessly while persevering agony and pain. *[32]

Granted, observing this foundational obligation in the manner beloved to Allāh, the Lord of the Worlds, mounts to fulfilling this religion's pillar. The Prophet (صَلَّى ٱللَّهُ عَلَيْهِ وَسَلَّمَ) said:

بُـنِـيَ الإِسْلَامُ عَلَى خَمْسٍ: شَهَادَةِ أَنْ لَا إِلَـهَ إِلَّا اللهُ، وَأَنَّ مُـحَمَّدًا رَسُولُ اللهِ، وَإِقَامِ الصَّلَاةِ، وَإِيتَاءِ الزَّكَاةِ، وَالْـحَجِّ، وَصَوْمِ رَمَضَانَ.

"Islām is built on five pillars: to testify that there is no god worthy of worship but Allāh and that Muḥammad is the

[32] This part is taken from a Friday sermon delivered on Ramaḍān 19th 1432 / 9/18/2011. It is titled "The bankrupt observant of fasting".

Messenger of Allāh, perform the prayer, give out Zakat, perform Hajj, and observe fasting."[33]

The soundness of this Ḥadīth is agreed upon by al-Bukhārī and Muslim.

Fasting properly requires drawing oneself to Allāh, the Lord of the worlds, through refraining from prohibited acts.

For example, the Messenger (صَلَّى ٱللَّهُ عَلَيْهِ وَسَلَّمَ) forbade perjury and speaking lies. He said,

مَنْ لَـمْ يَدَعْ قَوْلَ الزُّورِ، وَالْـعَمَلَ بِـهِ؛ فَلَيْـسَ للهِ حَاجَـةٌ فِي أَنْ يَدَعَ طَعَامَـهُ وَشَرَابَـهُ.

"If one does not eschew lies and false conduct, Allāh does not need that he should abstain from his food and his drink."[34]

Typically, one abstains from temporary prohibitions during fasting. Apart from the period of fasting, such temporary bans are made lawful by Allāh, the Lord of the worlds, such as food, drink, and lawful lust. However, during fasting, one should abstain from sexual intercourse and its means, such as misguided gazing and indulging prohibited acts. It is even more pressing that the individual should be very cautious in the face of modern-day tools such as the mobile phone, radio, television, and the internet. Of particular gravity, the internet is a severe trial, and people are as glued to it as idol worshippers. It devours their piety, robs them of their faith, and

---

[33] Recorded by al-Bukhārī in his Ṣaḥīḥ collection: (1/49) no. (8) and Muslim: (11/45) no. (16).

[34] Recorded by al-Bukhārī in his Ṣaḥīḥ collection: (4/116) no. (1903). He recorded another version of it that reads, "**If anyone does not eschew lies, false conduct, and foolish behavior**… (10/472) no. (6057)

teaches them lying, deceit, and hypocrisy. The individual should pay close attention to such emerging issues because they undoubtedly impact one's life, let alone his fasting.

When everyone fasts the whole month, they are doing so as one nation. They break their fast at the same time and abstain at the same time.

Well-off people will then realize the favor of Allāh, thus causing them to treat the poor with compassion. Fasting reduces the whispers and pitfalls schemed by Shaytān, who flows through the body of a human just like blood does, as indicated by the Messenger of Allāh (صَلَّىٱللَّهُعَلَيۡهِوَسَلَّمَ).[35]

Ramaḍān is the month of fasting and patience. It demands abstinence from lusts and desirable indulgences. The greater one's patience, the greater one's reward from Allāh Almighty. Allāh (جَلَّجَلَالُهُ) said:

﴿ إِنَّمَا يُوَفَّى ٱلصَّٰبِرُونَ أَجۡرَهُم بِغَيۡرِ حِسَابٖ ١٠ ﴾

> **"Only those who are patient shall receive their reward in full, without reckoning."** [Sūrah az-Zumar (39):10]

Allāh Almighty forgives the fasting persons. Abū Hurayrah (رَضِيَٱللَّهُعَنۡهُ) reported that the Messenger of Allāh (صَلَّىٱللَّهُعَلَيۡهِوَسَلَّمَ) said:

[35] Recorded by al-Bukhārī in his Ṣaḥīḥ collection: (4/278) no. (2035) and Muslim: (4/1712) no. (2715) on the authority of Ṣafiyya bint Ḥuyay (may Allāh be pleased with her).

الصَّلَوَاتُ الْـخَمْسُ، وَالْـجُمُعَةُ إِلَى الْـجُمُعَةِ، وَرَمَضَانُ إِلَى رَمَضَانَ
مُكَفِّرَاتٌ مَا بَيْنَـهُنَّ إِذَا اجْتُنِبَتِ الْـكَبَائِـرُ.

"The five daily (prescribed) prayers, and Friday (prayer) to the next Friday (prayer), and the fasting of Ramaḍān to the next Ramaḍān, is an expiation of the sins committed in between them, so long as major sins are avoided."[36] Recorded by Muslim.

Fasting prevents one from indulging in immoralities. Abū Hurayrah (رَضِيَ ٱللَّهُ عَنْهُ) reported that the Messenger of Allāh (صَلَّى ٱللَّهُ عَلَيْهِ وَسَلَّمَ) said:

الصِّيَامُ جُنَّـةٌ، فَلَا يَرْفُثْ وَلَا يَـجْهَلْ، وَإِنِ امْرُؤٌ قَاتَلَـهُ أَوْ شَاتَـمَـهُ؛
فَلْيَقُلْ إِنِّي صَائِـمٌ، إِنِّي صَائِـمٌ.

"fasting is a shield. When anyone of you is observing fast, one should neither indulge in obscene language nor should one raise his voice; and say, 'I am fasting, I am fasting."

One should say so twice as reported in the agreed-upon Ḥadīth.[37]

Allāh (تَبَارَكَ وَتَعَالَىٰ) tied acts of worship with prime objectives, some of which Allāh (سُبْحَانَهُ وَتَعَالَىٰ) taught us. When the individual engages in any act of worship, he complies with the commands of Allāh and expects a [handsome] reward for the toil he has undergone. For example, when fasting coincides with hot days, one has to endure thirst and hardship to secure a greater reward from Allāh, the Lord of the worlds.

---

[36] Recorded by Muslim in his Ṣaḥīḥ collection: (1/209) no. (233).
[37] Cited earlier.

Some of the objectives of fasting are known to us, while others remain beyond our knowledge. Yet, the underlying aim is to worship Allāh, the Lord of the worlds, by observing such acts of worship, which, by default, are a mystery to us. In other words, we worship Allāh without asking why. We should not as: why did Allāh obligate the observance of five daily prayers? Why had He not bound more or less? All we should care about is that Allāh (تَبَارَكَ وَتَعَالَى) mandated them.

Accordingly, the nonvisual should endeavor to improve his behavior and strives to perform any act of worship in the manner beloved to Allāh, the Lord of the worlds. Ultimately, we have to question ourselves. We must scour ourselves for the pitfalls that consume our hearts and souls so that we can get rid of them. Regardless of how plentiful one engages in good deeds, the fact that one's heart is blemished renders such good deeds unaccepted by Allāh, the Lord of the worlds. In contrast, a handful of good deeds observed with a sincere and honest self is sure to bring Allāh's pleasure. Allāh said:

﴿ إِنَّمَا يَتَقَبَّلُ ٱللَّهُ مِنَ ٱلْمُتَّقِينَ ٢٧ ﴾

"Verily, Allāh accepts only from those who are Al-Muttaqūn (the pious)." [Sūrah al-Māʾidah (5):27] * [38]

[38] This summary is taken from a lecture delivered on Monday Ramaḍān 1st 1432 / 8/1/2011.

THE CONDUCT OF THE PIOUS OBSERVANTS OF FASTING

As recorded by al-Bukhārī, Abū Hurayrah (رَضِيَ ٱللَّهُ عَنْهُ) reported that the Messenger of Allāh (صَلَّى ٱللَّهُ عَلَيْهِ وَسَلَّمَ) said:

مَنْ لَمْ يَدَعْ قَوْلَ الزُّورِ وَالْجَهْلَ وَالْعَمَلَ بِهِ، فَلَيْسَ للهِ حَاجَةٌ فِي أَنْ يَدَعَ طَعَامَهُ وَشَرَابَهُ.

"If one does not eschew lies and false conduct, Allāh does not need that he should abstain from his food and his drink."

In a sound narration recorded by ibn Māja[39], it reads:

مَنْ لَمْ يَدَعْ قَوْلَ الزُّورِ، وَالْجَهْلَ، وَالْعَمَلَ بِهِ؛ فَلَيْسَ للهِ حَاجَةٌ فِي أَنْ يَدَعَ طَعَامَهُ وَشَرَابَهُ.

"If one does not eschew lies, foolish behavior, and indulgence of such acts, Allāh does not need that he should abstain from his food and his drink."

Foolish behavior manifests in mischievousness, arrogance, and lack of reason. Abū Hurayrah (رَضِيَ ٱللَّهُ عَنْهُ) reported that the Messenger of Allāh (صَلَّى ٱللَّهُ عَلَيْهِ وَسَلَّمَ) said:

---

[39] Recorded in 'al-Sunan': (1/539) no. (1689).

رُبَّ صَائِـمٍ لَيْسَ لَـهُ مِنْ صِيَامِـهِ إِلَّا الْـجُوعُ وَالْعَطَشُ، وَرُبَّ قَائِـمٍ لَيْسَ لَـهُ مِنْ قِيَامِـهِ إِلَّا السَّهَرُ.

"There are people who fast and get nothing from their fast except hunger and thirst, and there are those who pray and get nothing from their prayer but a sleepless night."[40]

Recorded by ibn Māja and this Hadith is sound.

In an inclusive report, the Prophet (صَلَّى ٱللَّهُ عَلَيْهِ وَسَلَّمَ) concluded:

لَيْسَ الصِّيَامُ مِنَ الأَكْلِ وَالشُّرْبِ؛ إِنَّـمَا الصِّيَامُ مِنَ اللَّغْوِ والرَّفَثِ.

"Fasting is not meant to merely abstain from eating and drinking but rather to abstain from any unnecessary and obscene talk."[41]

It is recorded by ibn Khuzayma and ibn Ḥibbān on the authority of abū Hurayrah (رَضِيَ ٱللَّهُ عَنْهُ). It is also a sound hadith. * [42]

---

[40] Recoded by ibn Māja in 'al-Sunan': (1/539) no. (1690) and Ahmad in 'al-Musnad: (2/373) no. (8856). The above wording is Ahmad's. Ibn Māja's narration reads, "**There are people who fast and get nothing from their fast except hunger, and there are those who pray and get nothing from their prayer but a sleepless night**." This hadith's chain of transmission is good. Al-ʾAlbānī graded its content (*matn*) as sound in ʾṢaḥīḥ al-Targhīb wa al-Tarhībʾ: (1/625) no. (1083).

[41] Recorded by ibn Khuzayma in 'al-Ṣaḥīḥ': (3/242) no. (1996), ibn Ḥibbān in 'al-Ṣaḥīḥ' following the organization of ibn Bilbān: (8/255, 256) no. (3479), al-Ḥākim in 'al-Mustadrak': (1/430, 431) no. (1570), and al-Bayhaqī in 'al-Sunan al-Kubrā': (4/270) no. (8312). Al-ʾAlbānī graded this hadith as sound in 'ʾṢaḥīḥ al-Targhīb wa al-Tarhībʾ: (1/625) no. (1082).

[42] This part is taken from a lecture delivered on a Friday sermon Ramaḍān 19th 1432 / 8/19/ 2011. The title is "the bankrupt observants of fasting".

It is certain now that the observant of fasting must comply with the commands of Allāh and refrain from prohibited acts and utterances. For example, one must not backbite people, tell lies, gossip, or sell unlawful merchandise. Ideally, committing to this behavior for an entire month ensures straightforwardness throughout the rest of the year. Unfortunately, many of those who observe fasting do not distinguish between their regular day and fasting day. They follow their habit of disobeying the commands and engaging in prohibitions. It feels as if they lack the reverence imparted by fasting. Though such acts do not necessarily nullify one's fasting, they certainly decrease its reward, or worse, obliterate it all together when measured up.

Abū Hurayrah (رَضِيَٱللَّهُعَنْهُ) reported that the Messenger of Allāh (صَلَّىٱللَّهُعَلَيْهِوَسَلَّمَ) said:

كُلُّ عَمَلِ ابْنِ آدَمَ لَـهُ إِلَّا الصِّيَامَ، فَإِنَّـهُ لِي وَأَنَا أَجْزِي بِـهِ، وَالصِّيَامُ جُنَّـةٌ، فَإِذَا كَـانَ يَوْمُ صَوْمِ أَحَدِكُمْ؛ فَلَا يَـرْفُثْ وَلَا يَـصْخَبْ، فَإِنْ سَابَّـهُ أَحَدٌ أَوْ قَاتَـلَـهُ فَلْيَقُلْ: إِنِّـي صَائِـمٌ، إِنِّـي صَـائِـمٌ.

"Allāh Almighty said, 'Every act of the son of Adam is for him, except fasting, which is (exclusively) for Me, and I will reward him for it.' Fasting is a shield. When anyone of you is observing fast, he should neither indulge in obscene language nor should he raise his voice, and if anyone reviles him or tries to quarrel with him, he should say: 'I am fasting."

This version is recorded by al-Bukhārī. Muslim and others also record the Ḥadīth.

Abū Hurayrah (رَضِيَٱللَّهُعَنْهُ) reported that the Messenger of Allāh (صَلَّىٱللَّهُعَلَيْهِوَسَلَّمَ) said:

لَيْسَ الصِّيَامُ مِنَ الْأَكْلِ وَالشُّرْبِ، إِنَّمَا الصِّيَامُ مِنَ اللَّغْوِ وَالرَّفَثِ؛ فَإِنْ سَابَّكَ أَحَدٌ أَوْ جَهِلَ عَلَيْكَ فَقُلْ: إِنِّي صَائِمٌ، إِنِّي صَائِمٌ.

"Fasting is not meant to merely abstain from eating and drinking but rather to abstain from any unnecessary and obscene talk. If someone were to insult or quarrel with you, say, 'I am fasting, I am fasting."

Recorded by ibn Khuzayma, ibn Ḥibbān, and al-Ḥākim. It is a sound hadith.

In another version recorded by ibn Khuzayma, the Prophet (صَلَّىٱللَّهُعَلَيْهِوَسَلَّمَ) said:

لَا تَسَابَّ وَأَنْتَ صَائِمٌ، فَإِنْ سَابَّكَ أَحَدٌ فَقُلْ: إِنِّي صَائِمٌ، وَإِنْ كُنْتَ قَائِمًا فَاجْلِسْ.

"Do not insult one another while fasting. If someone were to insult you, say, 'I am fasting; and sit down if you were standing."

This Hadith is graded as good (ḥasan). * [43]

Servants of Allāh, genuine worship to Allāh, will drive the individual to do good deeds, embody upright morals, kindness to people, and abstention from harming others. Failing to achieve any

[43] This part is taken from a Friday sermon delivered on Sha`ban 25th 1436 / 6/12/2015. The title is "Inviting the brothers to repent in Ramaḍān".

of this through worship means that it is void of goodness and would not benefit its observer.

As recorded in *Ṣaḥīḥ al-`Adab al-Mufrad*[44], abū Hurayrah (رَضِيَٱللَّهُعَنْهُ) reported that the Messenger of Allāh (صَلَّىٱللَّهُعَلَيْهِوَسَلَّمَ) was asked:

قِيلَ لِلنَّبِيِّ (صَلَّى اللهُ عَلَيْهِ وَسَلَّمَ): يَا رَسُولَ اللهِ! إِنَّ فُلَانَـةَ تَقُومُ اللَّيْلِ، وَتَصُومُ النَّهَارَ، وَتَفْعَلُ، وَتَصَّدَّقُ، وَتُؤْذِي جِيرَانَهَا بِلِسَانِهَا؟ فَقَالَ رَسُولُ اللهِ (صَلَّى اللهُ عَلَيْهِ وَسَلَّمَ): لَا خَيْرَ فِيهَا، هِيَ مِنْ أَهْلِ النَّارِ.

> **"Messenger of Allāh, so and so female spends the night in prayer, fasts during the day, does other good deeds, and give out charity in abundance, but harms her neighbors with foul language.' The Messenger of Allāh (صَلَّىٱللَّهُعَلَيْهِوَسَلَّمَ) replied: "She is void of any good, and she is among the inhabitants of the hellfire."**

As described in the Ḥadīth, she spends the night in prayer, fasts during the day, and does all sorts of good deeds, in addition to giving out charity. Interestingly, the type of charity she is giving out has not been named in the Hadith, which implies she gives out abundantly. However, she still harms her neighbors with foul language. The Messenger of Allāh (صَلَّىٱللَّهُعَلَيْهِوَسَلَّمَ) set the record straight:

لَا خَيْرَ فِيهَا، هِيَ مِنْ أَهْلِ النَّارِ.

[44] Ṣaḥīḥ al-`Adab al-Mufrad: (69) no. (88). It is also recorded by Ahmad in 'al-Musnad': (2/440) no. (9675), al-Bukhārī in 'al-Adab al-Mufrad': (41) no. (119). This hadith is graded as sound by al-`Albānī in also his other book 'al-Ṣaḥīḥ': (1/369) no. (190).

"she is void of any good, and she is among the inhabitants of the hellfire."

The countless days she fasted, the countless nights she spent praying, and the abundance of good deeds and charity are thrown out because they have not produced any value. Even though she did all of this, she spoke to her neighbors with foul language.

The Ḥadīth continues,

وَفُلَانَـةُ تُصَلِّي الْـمَكْتُوبَـةَ، وَتَصَّدَّقُ بِأَثْوَارٍ-جَمْعُ ثَوْرٍ، وَهِيَ الْقِطْعَةُ مِنَ الْـجُبْنِ الْـمُجَفَّفِ- وَتَصَّدَّقُ بِأَثْوَارٍ -وَالتَّنْوِينُ فِي ((بِأَثْوَارٍ)) لِلتَّقْلِيلِ- وَتَصَّدَّقُ بِأَثْوَارٍ، وَلَا تُؤْذِي أَحَدًا؟. قَالَ (صَلَّى اللهُ عَلَيْهِ وَسَلَّمَ): هِيَ مِنْ أَهْلِ الْـجَنَّـةِ.

"Another female observes the five obligated prayers, give out some pieces of dried cheese in charity, and harms no one." The Messenger of Allāh (صَلَّى ٱللَّهُ عَلَيْهِ وَسَلَّمَ) replied, "She is among the inhabitants of paradise."

How vast the gap between the first and the second instance is the [impact] of worship. One example shows worship that drives good conduct, whereas another act of worship fails to prevent the individual from excessive evil. The first instance shows a woman who moderated herself through night prayer and fasting yet could not straighten up her tongue or refrain from harming people. Indeed, how wide a gap between both acts of worship; and how pitiful the bankrupt observant of fasting. *[45]

[45] This part is taken from a lecture delivered on a Friday sermon Ramaḍān 19th 1432 / 8/19/ 2011. The title is "the bankrupt observants of fasting".

THE BANKRUPT OBSERVANTS OF FASTING

As recorded in Ṣaḥīḥ Muslim, Abū Hurayrah (رَضِيَٱللَّهُعَنْهُ) reported that the Messenger of Allāh (صَلَّىٱللَّهُعَلَيْهِوَسَلَّمَ) said:

إِنَّ الْمُفْلِسَ مِنْ أُمَّتِي يَأْتِي يَوْمَ الْقِيَامَةِ بِصَلاَةٍ وَصِيَامٍ وَزَكَاةٍ وَيَأْتِي قَدْ شَتَمَ هَذَا وَقَذَفَ هَذَا وَأَكَلَ مَالَ هَذَا وَسَفَكَ دَمَ هَذَا وَضَرَبَ هَذَا فَيُعْطَى هَذَا مِنْ حَسَنَاتِهِ وَهَذَا مِنْ حَسَنَاتِهِ فَإِنْ فَنِيَتْ حَسَنَاتُهُ قَبْلَ أَنْ يُقْضَى مَا عَلَيْهِ أُخِذَ مِنْ خَطَايَاهُمْ فَطُرِحَتْ عَلَيْهِ ثُمَّ طُرِحَ فِي النَّارِ

"Do you know who is the bankrupt? They (the Companions of the Prophet) replied, "The bankrupt man amongst us has neither dirham nor wealth.' He (the Prophet) said, "The bankrupt of my nation would be the one to come on the Day of Judgment with much prayers and days of Fasting and Zakat but (he would find himself bankrupt on that day as he would have exhausted his funds of virtues) since he hurled abuses upon others, slandered others and unlawfully consumed the wealth of others and shed the blood of others and assaulted others. His good deeds would be credited to the account of one (who suffered at his hand). And if his good deeds fall short of clearing the account, then his sins would be entered in (his account), and he would be thrown in the Hell-Fire."[46]

[46] Recorded by Muslim: (4/1997) no. (2581).

The person described here prays, fasts, and gives out Zakat regularly but simultaneously perpetrated what exhausted his funds of good to the extent it eradicated it. If we look closely, five offenses are listed in the Hadith: abuse, slander, unlawful consumption of others' wealth, killing, and assault. So, if he had time to commit all of these offenses, when did he actually fast? How did he find time to perform prayer amidst all of those crimes? Could he be a payer of Zakat though consume the wealth of others unlawfully? What kind of fasting did he do? What are the things he abstained from?

It is indeed unsettling to find a person consumed with all of these crimes yet finds time to perform the prayer. True fasting, perfect prayer, and acceptable Zakat run interference when one decides to engage in the above five crimes. Ungenuine performance of those acts would not intervene in this decision because the Messenger of Allāh (صَلَّى ٱللَّٰهُ عَلَيْهِ وَسَلَّمَ) indicated that such person actually pray, fast, and give out Zakat. Still, they have not stopped him from committing those crimes. Had he observed true fasting, performed perfect prayer, and gave out acceptable Zakat, he would have halted himself before committing those offenses and committed to the straight path of Allāh.

The Messenger of Allāh (صَلَّى ٱللَّٰهُ عَلَيْهِ وَسَلَّمَ) pointed out true bankruptcy. In short, **it is the moral bankruptcy in this life** because it leads to eventual bankruptcy in the Hereafter. It exhausts the funds of good deeds and relocates the victims' sins to the perpetrator's account so that he is eventually thrown into Hellfire. * [47]

[47] This part is taken from a lecture delivered on a Friday sermon Ramaḍān 19th 1432 / 8/19/ 2011. The title is "the bankrupt observants of fasting".

BEWARE OF SINNING IN PRIVATE

In a sound *Isnād* (chain of transmission), ibn Mājah[48] recorded on the authority of Thawbān (may Allāh be pleased with him) who reported that the Prophet (peace and blessings be upon him) said,

لَأَعْلَمَنَّ أَقْوَامًا مِنْ أُمَّتِي يَأْتُونَ يَوْمَ الْقِيَامَةِ بِحَسَنَاتٍ أَمْثَالِ جِبَالِ تِهَامَةَ بِيضًا فَيَجْعَلُهَا اللَّهُ عَزَّ وَجَلَّ هَبَاءً مَنْثُورًا

"I certainly know people of my nation who will come on the Day of Judgment with good, white deeds like the mountains of *Tihāma*, but Allāh will make them like scattered dust."

This Hadith presents us with an example of hardworking people. On the Day of Judgment, their deeds are as enormous as the mountains of Tihama, which is a mountain range extending far and wide. Those good deeds weigh so heavily, as suggested by the Hadith. Indeed, producing such an enormous number of good deeds is extraordinary, but, unfortunately, Allāh will make them like scattered dust. Those hardworking individuals are good-doers who spare no effort to achieve righteousness, as proven by the massive number of good deeds they bear on the Day of Judgment. Thawbān (رَضِيَ اللَّهُ عَنْهُ) asked,

"O Messenger of Allāh, describe them to us and tell us more, lest we be like them unknowingly.'"

This part reflects how the Companions were afraid of failing to detect any potential threat that may doom their

48 Ibn Māja recorded it in 'al-Sunan': (2/1418) no. (4245). The Isnad of this hadith is graded as sound by al-'Albānī in his book 'al-Ṣaḥīḥ': (2/32) no. (505).

good deeds to unacceptance. It also proves that the individual may be deceived into believing he is a good person when, in fact, he is not. Allāh said:

﴿ وَهُمْ يَحْسَبُونَ أَنَّهُمْ يُحْسِنُونَ صُنْعًا ﴿١٠٤﴾ ﴾

"whose efforts in this world are misguided, even when they think they are doing good work?" [Sūrah al-Kahf (18):104]

The Messenger of Allāh (ﷺ) said:

أَمَا إِنَّهُمْ إِخْوَانُكُمْ، وَمِنْ جِلْدَتِكُمْ، وَيَأْخُذُونَ مِنَ اللَّيْلِ كَمَا تَأْخُذُونَ؛ وَلَكِنَّهُمْ أَقْوَامٌ إِذَا خَلَوْا بِمَحَارِمِ اللهِ انْتَهَكُوهَا.

"They are your brothers and from your ethnicity, worshipping at night as you do, but they will be people who, when they are alone, transgress the sacred limits of Allāh."

"**Worshipping at night as you do":** It means they endure the hardship of standing up to pray, recite, kneel, prostrate, and supplicate during the night.

Sinning in private is the fatal downfall that voided all this hard work. It seemed integrated and powerful at face value, but this downfall ate it up from the inside, leading to its collapse and decline. In public, such people project a healthy image, but behind the curtain, they are faulted, in the same way as a grave, attracting from the outside but containing a filthy corpse. Transgressing the limits of Allāh is compelling proof of the corruption and futility of one's devotion because it indicates a corrupted self, loss of righteousness, and defiance of Allāh's limits. In short, all add up to a faulted faith.

Allāh said:

﴿ وَتِلْكَ حُدُودُ ٱللَّهِ ۗ وَلِلْكَٰفِرِينَ عَذَابٌ أَلِيمٌ ﴿٤﴾ ﴾

"These are the limits set by Allâh. And for disbelievers, there is a painful torment." [Sūrah al-Mujaadilah (58):4]

And,

﴿ وَمَن يَتَعَدَّ حُدُودَ ٱللَّهِ فَأُوْلَٰٓئِكَ هُمُ ٱلظَّٰلِمُونَ ﴿٢٢٩﴾ ﴾

"And whoever transgresses the limits ordained by Allāh, then such are the Zâlimûn (wrong-doers)." [Sūrah al-Baqarah (2):229]

And,

﴿ وَتِلْكَ حُدُودُ ٱللَّهِ يُبَيِّنُهَا لِقَوْمٍ يَعْلَمُونَ ﴿٢٣٠﴾ ﴾

"These are Allāh's bounds, which He makes clear for those who know." [Sūrah al-Baqarah (2):230]

If the transgressors of Allāh's limits lose the traits of fairness, knowledge, and faith, what good deeds do they have left?! Even worse, what sense of religiousness do they have left?!

أُولَئِكَ قَوْمٌ إِذَا خَلَوْا بِمَحَارِمِ اللهِ انْتَهَكُوهَا

"People who, when they are alone, transgress the sacred limits of Allāh."

This statement proves their lack of having Taqwā of Allāh. Accordingly, the public good deeds are meant to attract people's admiration, extra attention, and status elevation beyond their rightful place. One should be very mindful of himself in three instances,

إِذَا عَمِلْتَ فَاذْكُرْ نَظَرَ اللهِ إِلَيْكَ، وَإِذَا تَكَلَّمْتَ فَاذْكُرْ سَمْعَ اللهِ مِنْكَ، وَإِذَا سَكَتَّ فَاذْكُرْ عِلْمَ اللهِ فِيكَ.

> **"Allāh is watching when one does a good deed; Allāh is listening when one speaks; Allāh knows everything about oneself even when one remains silent,"[49]**

Sufyan noted,

مَا عَالَجْتُ شَيْئًا أَشَدَّ عَلَيَّ مِنْ نَفْسِي؛ مَرَّةً عَلَيَّ، وَمَرَّةً لِي.

> **"Nothing was more strenuous to me than having to struggle with myself; we would take turns winning."[50]**

As you see, one sometimes wins but loses to himself other times. Life, in general, is nothing but toiling, laboring, affliction, and perseverance. It flashes a glimpse of happiness, only to follow through with distress. In a word, this is LIFE. It will not last. Allāh Almighty said:

---

[49] Recorded by abu Nu`aym in 'Ḥilyat al-'Awliyā'': (8/75) biography number (396). It is also recorded by 'Ismā'īl ibn Muḥammad al-'Aṣbahānī in 'Siyar al-Salaf al-Ṣāliḥīn': (1101) biography number (358). This statement is made by Ḥātim al-'Aṣṣam (may Allāh have mercy upon him).

[50] Recorded by abu Nu`aym in 'Ḥilyat al-'Awliyā'': (7/5, 62) under the biography of Sufyān al-Thawrī (395) and al-Khāṭīb in 'al-Jāmi' li Akhlāq al-Rāwī: (1/317) no. (692). Its chain of transmission is sound. One version of this statement reads, "Nothing was more strenuous to me than having to struggle with my intention, as it was in constant change."

﴿ وَإِنَّ ٱلدَّارَ ٱلْءَاخِرَةَ لَهِىَ ٱلْحَيَوَانُۚ لَوْ كَانُوا۟ يَعْلَمُونَ ﴿٦٤﴾ ﴾

"the true life is in the Hereafter, if only they knew." [Sūrah al-ʿAnkabūt (29):64]

The lasting life is in the Hereafter; so, put forth good deeds for that life and beware of the vanishing one. Indeed, had been this world made of perishing gold and the Hereafter from pottery, the afterlife would edge out this world. But the fact is that this world is made of perishing pottery, whereas the Hereafter is made of lasting gold.

Maymūn ibn Mahrān remarked,

لَا يَكُونُ الرَّجُلُ تَقِيًّا حَتَّى يَكُونَ لِنَفْسِهِ أَشَدَّ مُحَاسَبَةً مِنَ الشَّرِيكِ لِشَرِيكِهِ، وَحَتَّى يَعْلَمَ مِنْ أَيْنَ مَلْبَسُهُ وَمَطْعَمُهُ وَمَشْرَبُهُ؛ فَلْيَنْظُرْ مَا يَدْخُلُ بَطْنَهُ.

"A man is not yet pious unless he holds himself into account far relentless than partners to one another and has exact knowledge of the source of his food, drink, and clothing to have a record of everything he consumes."[51]

These criteria are the most formidable to ascertain one's Taqwā of Allāh.

On one occasion, one of the early scholars happened to live in an area notoriously known for unlawful activities. He entered the

---

[51] Recorded by Wakīʿ in 'al-Zuhd': (501, 502) no. (239), ibn abū Shayba in 'al-Muṣnnaf': (13/519; 14/36), Hanād ibn al-Sirrī in 'al-Zuhd': (2/580) no. (1228), ibn abū al-Dunyā in 'Muhasabat al-Nafs' as part of his Hadith encyclopedia: (5/284) no. (7), and abū Nuʿaym in 'Ḥilyat al-ʿAwliyā': (4/89) biography no. (251). The chain of transmission of this report is sound.

Masjid therein. After the prayer was announced, people jostled one another to stand in the first row. This scholar advised them:

كُلْ مِنْ حَلَالٍ، وَصَلِّ فِي الصَّفِّ الْأَخِيرِ

"Earn your income from lawful means, and you do not have to jostle for standing in the first row."[52]

This advice is basically meant to encourage watchfulness of one's source of income. As for competing to stand in the first row, the Messenger of Allāh (ﷺ) exhibited the excellence of such endeavor:

وَلَوْ عَلِمَ النَّاسُ مَا فِي النِّدَاءِ وَالصَّفِّ الْأَوَّلِ، ثُمَّ لَمْ يَجِدُوا إِلَّا أَنْ يَسْتَهِمُوا-أَيْ يَقْتَرِعُوا-عَلَيْهِمَا؛ لَفَعَلُوا.

"If people came to know the blessing of calling Adhan and the standing in the first row, they could do nothing but would draw lots to secure these privileges."[53]

What the early scholar meant was wondering why people have inverted the measures. They jostle one another to secure such an

---

[52] Recorded by al-Bayhaqī in 'Shu'ab al-'Īmān': (7/514) no. (5393) with a sound chain of transmission. Al-Fuḍayl ibn 'Iyāḍ reported, "A man asked Sufyān al-Thawrī about the excellence of standing at the first row. He told him, "Pay close attention to the source of your food [whether unlawful or unlawful]; and you do not have to jostle for standing in the first row." In another narration, Shu`ayb ibn Ḥarb said, "Sufyān al-Thawrī gave an advice that reads, 'Investigate the source of your income [whether lawful or unlawful] and you do not have to jostle for standing in the first row." This report's chain of transmission is sound. 'Shu'ab al-'Īmān': (7/514, 515) no. (5394). Ḥudhayfa al-Mur'ishī (may Allāh have mercy upon him) is reported to have made a statement on the same lines.

[53] Recorded by al-Bukhārī in his Ṣaḥīḥ collection: (2/96) no. (615) and Muslim: (1/235) no. (437) on the authority of abū Huraira (may Allāh be pleased with him).

easy goal while neglecting one of most critical obligations, namely to have Taqwā of Allāh Almighty regarding the source of their income. Each one must be mindful of everything that goes into our mouths because the body is the first thing to decay after one's death.

لَا يَكُونُ الرَّجُلُ تَقِيًّا حَتَّى يَكُونَ لِنَفْسِهِ أَشَدَّ مُحَاسَبَةً مِنَ الشَّرِيكِ لِشَرِيكِهِ.

"A man is not yet pious unless he holds himself into account far relentless than partners to one another."

Your self is your opponent, and you must drive it persistently to fulfill Allāh's due right and avoid what He prohibits. If you fail, your self will drive you around to fulfill its evil desires.

Bilal ibn Sa`d noted,

لَا تَكُنْ وَلِيًّا للهِ فِي الْعَلَانِيَةِ، عَدُوًّا للهِ فِي السِّرِّ.

"Do not pretend to have Taqwā of Allāh in public yet an enemy of Him in private."[54]

As mentioned in the previous Ḥadīth:

أُولَئِكَ قَوْمٌ إِذَا خَلَوْا بِمَحَارِمِ اللهِ انْتَهَكُوهَا.

54 Recorded by ibn abū al-Dunyā in 'al-'Ikhlāṣ' as part of his Hadith encyclopedia: (1/42) no. (26), al-Firyābī in 'Ṣifat al-Nifāq': (125) no. (85), abū Nu`aym in 'Ḥilyat al-'Awliyā': (5/228) biography no. (319), and ibn 'Asākir in 'Tārīkh Dimashq': (10/488) biography no. (975). This report's chain of transmission is sound.

"People who, when they are alone, transgress the sacred limits of Allāh."

The people who do an enormous number of good deeds in par with the *Tihama* mountain range have Taqwā of Allāh in public. Even their good deeds are described as "**white,**" but, in private, they are the enemies of Allāh.

Turning to fasting, it should inherit have Taqwā of Allāh Almighty and the righteousness of the heart. ʿAbd al-ʿAzīz ibn Abū Rawwād said:

أَدْرَكْتُـهُمْ يَـجْتَهِدُونَ فِي الْعَمَلِ الصَّالِـحِ، فَإِذَا فَعَلُوهُ؛ وَقَعَ عَلَيْهِمُ الْـهَـمُّ -لِمَ وَقَدْ عَمِلُوا صَالِـحًا؟! بَلْ عَمِلُوا صَالِـحًا اجْتَهَدُوا فِـي عَمَلِهِ-، يَقُولُ: أَدْرَكْتُـهُمْ يَـجْتَهِدُونَ فِـي الْعَمَلِ الصَّالِحِ، فَإِذَا فَعَلُوهُ؛ وَقَعَ عَلَيْهِمُ الْـهَمُّ؛ أَيُقْبَـلُ مِنْهُمْ أَمْ لَا؟!.

> **"I lived to witness them do good deeds. Once done, they are overwhelmed with distress. "Why would they sustain such feeling after striving to do good deeds? He continues, "Once done, they are overwhelmed with distress; would those good deeds be accepted or not?"[55]**

What counts is not the multitude of good deeds but rather purifying the good deeds of any blemishes. In other words, actions have consequences; blemishing the acts causes unfavorable repercussions, whereas cleansing them causes a favorable outcome. Only those lacking sincerity are tripped in obstacles.

Ali (may Allāh be pleased with him) said,

---

[55] Listed by ibn Rajab in 'Laṭā'if al-Maʿārif': (376).

كُونُوا لِقَبُولِ الْعَمَلِ أَشَدَّ اهْتِمَامًا مِنْكُمْ بِالْعَمَلِ، أَلَمْ تَسْمَعُوا اللهَ (عَزَّ وَجَلَّ) يَقُولُ: ﴿ إِنَّمَا يَتَقَبَّلُ ٱللَّهُ مِنَ ٱلْمُتَّقِينَ ﴿٢٧﴾ ﴾

"Be more eager for the acceptance of your good deeds than for the deed itself. Have you not heard the saying of Allāh Almighty, "Verily, Allâh accepts only from those who are Al-Muttaqûn (the pious)."? [Sūrah Al-Māʾidah (5): 27]"[56]

As recorded by ibn Mājah in his book al-Sunan,

لَمَّا سَمِعَتْ عَائِشَةُ (رَضِيَ اللهُ عَنْهَا) قَوْلَ اللهِ جَلَّ وَعَلَا: ﴿ وَٱلَّذِينَ يُؤْتُونَ مَآ ءَاتَواْ وَّقُلُوبُهُمْ وَجِلَةٌ أَنَّهُمْ إِلَىٰ رَبِّهِمْ رَٰجِعُونَ ﴿٦٠﴾ ﴾ فَقَالَتْ: يَا رَسُولَ اللهِ! أُولَئِكَ الْعُصَاةُ السَّرَقَةُ الزُّنَاةُ! يَفْعَلُونَ وَيَفْعَلُونَ؟ قَالَ: لَا يَا بِنْتَ الصِّدِّيقِ؛ بَلْ هُوَ الرَّجُلُ يَصُومُ، وَيُصَلِّي، وَيَتَصَدَّقُ، وَيَفْعَلُ الْخَيْرَ، وَيَخْشَى أَلَّا يُقْبَلَ مِنْهُ.

when ʿĀʾisha (may Allāh be pleased with her) heard the saying of Allāh Almighty,

"who always give with hearts that tremble at the thought that they must return to Him." [Sūrah Al-Mu`minūn (23): 60] She asked the Messenger of Allāh, "Does it refer to the disobedient, thieves, and the adulterers who are indulged in plenty of sins." He replied,

---

[56] Recorded by ibn abū al-Dunyā in 'al-ʾIkhlāṣ' as part of his Hadith encyclopedia: (1/39) no. (10). This report's chain of transmission is sound.

"No, daughter of al-Siddīq [i.e., Abū Bakr]. It actually refers to an individual who fasts, observes prayer, gives out charity, and does plenty of other good deeds while fear his actions may be rejected."[57]

Is there anyone capable of pinpointing the deep-rooted motives behind his actions? Who can ascertain the truth of his intentions definitively? Such a thing is known only to Allāh. Therefore, Ali (may Allāh be pleased with him) said,

كُونُوا لِقَبُولِ الْعَمَلِ أَشَدَّ اهْتِمَامًا مِنْكُمْ بِالْعَمَلِ، أَلَـمْ تَسْمَعُوا اللهَ (عَزَّ وَجَلَّ) يَقُولُ: ﴿ إِنَّمَا يَتَقَبَّلُ ٱللَّهُ مِنَ ٱلْمُتَّقِينَ ٢٧ ﴾

"Be more eager for the acceptance of your good deeds than for the deed itself. Have you not heard the saying of Allāh Almighty, "Verily, Allâh accepts only from those who are Al-Muttaqûn (the pious)."? [Sūrah Al-Mā'idah (5):27]" *[58]

[57] Recorded by al-Tirmidhī in 'al-Jāmi': (5/327, 328) no. (3175) and ibn Māja in 'al-Sunnan': (2/1404) no. (4198). Through gathering all the parallel versions of this hadith, al-'Albānī graded it as sound in 'al-Ṣaḥīḥa': (1/304) no. (162).

[58] This part is taken from a lecture delivered on a Friday sermon Ramaḍān 19th 1432 / 8/19/ 2011. The title is "the bankrupt observants of fasting".

FULFILLING THE OBJECTIVE OF FASTING: HAVE TAQWĀ OF ALLĀH

By virtue of Allāh's mercy, might, and power, let us fulfill fasting's underlying objective, namely developing have Taqwā of Allāh through sincere devotion to Allāh alone. This matter is achieved by complying with the commands and refraining from the prohibitions. This matter sums up having Taqwā of Allāh and the underlying objective of fasting.

We cannot and should not be that person the Messenger (صَلَّىٰ ٱللَّٰهُ عَلَيْهِ وَسَلَّمَ) described, who gains nothing from fasting but the suffering hunger and thirst. Even when he stands during the night to pray, he only has to endure toil and late nights. True fasting is not about abstaining from eating or drinking but rather refraining from idle and obscene talk and any other prohibition. It requires obeying the commands Allāh Almighty ordained and sent down in revelation on the chief of humans (صَلَّىٰ ٱللَّٰهُ عَلَيْهِ وَسَلَّمَ).

We ask Allāh, the Lord of the world, to provide us with the strength to muster the fast of Ramaḍān and standing in prayer in the manner beloved to Him; for He, Almighty is indeed the Most Generous, Most Kind, and Most Merciful.*[59]

[59] This part is taken from a Friday sermon delivered on Sha`ban 25th 1436 / 6/12/2015. The title is "Inviting the brothers to repent in Ramaḍān".

HOW DO WE LIVE RAMAḌĀN?

How do we live and enliven Ramaḍān?

A righteous person would receive Ramaḍān with sincere and consistent repentance. Such a person would entertain an uncompromising resolve to seize the opportunity of the month of Ramaḍān without wasting any second of it. Each individual should strive to fill his schedule with good deeds because none has any idea whether he will be alive or dead when Ramaḍān comes next year.

There are plenty of good deeds in Ramaḍān by which one seeks the cause of the Most Compassionate and Most Merciful:

Firstly Fasting:

The Prophet (peace and blessings be upon him) said,

مَنْ صَامَ رَمَضَانَ إِيمَانًا وَاحْتِسَابًا؛ غُفِرَ لَـهُ مَا تَقَدَّمَ مِنْ ذَنْبِـهِ

> **"Anyone fasts Ramaḍān out of faith and in the hope of Allāh's [reward] will have all of his past sins forgiven."**

The Ḥadīth is recorded in both Ṣaḥīḥ collections.

Fasting commands abstaining food as well as unlawful acts, all the more reason one must refrain from falsehood, lying, backbiting, and gossiping. There should be a difference between one's regular day and the day he fasts to gain nothing but the suffering of hunger and thirst. In short, fasting is the ultimate good deed in Ramaḍān.

Secondly, *Tarāwīh* prayer:

The Messenger of Allāh (صَلَّى اللَّهُ عَلَيْهِ وَسَلَّمَ) said:

مَنْ قَامَ رَمَضَانَ إِيمانًا وَاحْتِسَابًا؛ غُفِرَ لَـهُ مَا تَقَدَّمَ مِنْ ذَنْبِـهِ.

"Whosoever performs (optional *Ṭarāwīḥ*) prayers at night during the month of Ramaḍān, with Faith and in the hope of receiving Allāh's reward, will have his past sins forgiven."

Thirdly, Giving out charity:

It is one of this month's most encouraging deeds. Ibn `Abbās (رَضِيَٱللَّهُعَنْهُ) said:

كَـانَ رَسُولُ اللهِ صَلَّى اللهُ عَلَيْهِ وَسَلَّمَ أَجْوَدَ النَّاسِ بِالْـخَيْرِ، وَكَـانَ أَجْوَدَ مَا يَـكُونُ فِي رَمَضَانَ.

"The Messenger of Allāh (صَلَّىٱللَّهُعَلَيْهِوَسَلَّمَ) was the most generous and kindest of people, and he was even more so during Ramaḍān."

The Prophet (صَلَّىٱللَّهُعَلَيْهِوَسَلَّمَ) encouraged feeding a fasting person, inviting people to eat, and provide water. He (صَلَّىٱللَّهُعَلَيْهِوَسَلَّمَ) said:

مَنْ فَـطَّـرَ صَائِـمًا كَـانَ لَـهُ مِثْـلُ أَجْرِهِ غَيْـرَ أَنَّـهُ لَا يَنْقُصُ مِنْ أَجْرِ الصَّائِـمِ شَيْئًا.

"He who provides a fasting person something with which to break his fast will earn the same reward as the one who was observing the fast, without diminishing in any way the reward of the latter."

As recorded in the two Ṣaḥīḥ collections, `Abdullah ibn `Amr (رَضِيَ اللَّهُ عَنْهُ) reported that a man asked the Messenger of Allāh (صَلَّى اللَّهُ عَلَيْهِ وَسَلَّمَ): "What are the best of Islām's teachings?" He replied:

تُطْعِمُ الطَّعَامَ، وَتَقْرَأُ السَّلَامَ عَلَى مَنْ عَرَفْتَ وَمَنْ لَمْ تَعْرِفْ

"To feed people and greet anyone you know or do not know."

ʿUmar (رَضِيَ اللَّهُ عَنْهُ) reported that the Prophet (صَلَّى اللَّهُ عَلَيْهِ وَسَلَّمَ) was asked, "What are the best of good deeds?" He replied,

إِدْخَالُكَ السُّرُورَ عَلَى مُؤْمِنٍ، أَشْبَعْتَهُ مِنْ جُوعٍ، كَسَوْتَهُ مِنْ عُرْيٍ، قَضَيْتَ لَهُ حَاجَةً، أَعَنْتَهُ، فَرَّجْتَ لَهُ كُرْبًا بِإِذْنِ رَبِّهِ.

"To deliver good news to a fellow believer, supply food for the hungry, cloth the undressed, fulfill people's needs, and alleviate their distress by the will of their Lord."

It is recorded by al-Ṭabarānī in ʾal-ʾAwsaṭʾ using a good chain of transmission.

The Messenger of Allāh (صَلَّى اللَّهُ عَلَيْهِ وَسَلَّمَ) said:

فِي كُلِّ ذَاتِ كَبِدٍ حَرَّى أَجْرٌ

"There is a reward for [quenching the thirst] of every living being."

It is recorded by Ahmad using a sound chain of transmission. Quenching the thirst of any living being, even if it was a straying dog, is rewarded by Allāh.

A Muslim may designate a well or a water fountain for the thirst and the wanderer to drink from. Granted, water pollution is a common phenomenon that causes lethal ailments detrimental to the body. So, if anyone intends to build or designate such a place, he should do his best to keep it afar from any source of pollution. In this manner, that individual is included in the reward assigned in the Hadith for whoever put forth the best deed any servant could present before his Lord.

Fourthly, Recitation of the Qur᾽ān:

It is one of the good deeds to observe during the month of Ramaḍān. Gabriel used to recite the Qur᾽ān with the Prophet (peace and blessings be upon him) every Ramaḍān. Likewise, the Salaf used to dedicate their time to the recitation of the Book of Allāh, the Lord of the worlds, during Ramaḍān.

Fifthly, Sitting in the Masjid until sunset:

This good deed is advisable during Ramaḍān as well as the rest of the year. Anas (رَضِيَ ٱللَّهُ عَنْهُ) reported that the Prophet (صَلَّى ٱللَّهُ عَلَيْهِ وَسَلَّمَ) said:

مَنْ صَلَّى الْفَجْرَ فِي جَمَاعَةٍ، ثُمَّ قَعَدَ يَذْكُرُ اللهَ حَتَّى تَطْلُعَ الشَّمْسُ، ثُمَّ صَلَّى رَكْعَتَيْنِ؛ كَانَتْ لَهُ كَأَجْرِ حَجَّةٍ وَعُمْرَةٍ تَامَّةٍ تَامَّةٍ تَامَّةٍ.

> **"Anyone who performs the Fajr prayer in congregation stays sitting and remembering Allāh until the sunset, and then offers two Rak`as will the reap a reward equal to a complete Hajj and `Umrah."**

Al-Tirmidhī records this Ḥadīth which is graded as *ḥasan li Ghayrih* (suitable for extraneous reasons). This reward is assigned for any day of the year, let alone during Ramaḍān.

Sixthly, *Al-'I`tikāf* (seclusion in the Masjid):

"The Prophet (صَلَّى ٱللَّهُ عَلَيْهِ وَسَلَّمَ) was used to make *Al-'I`tikāf* ten days in every Ramaḍān. At the year of his death, he did so for twenty days."

Al-'I`tikāf is inclusive of many forms of worship such as Qur'ān recitation, prayer, and the remembrance of Allāh among others. It is best observed during the last ten days of Ramaḍān in the hope of seizing the *Night of al-Qadr*. It is a lawful seclusion meant to keep one's distance from people, family, friends, and children, only to draw oneself closer to Allāh, the Lord of the worlds. The person performing *Al-'I`tikāf* keeps himself away from everything but the worship of Allāh and cuts off any distraction that may disrupt his dedication to Allāh.

Seventhly, `Umrah:

The Messenger of Allāh (صَلَّى ٱللَّهُ عَلَيْهِ وَسَلَّمَ) said:

عُمْرَةٌ فِـي رَمَضَانَ كَحَجَّةٍ مَعِي

"Performing `Umrah in Ramaḍān equals the performance of Hajj with me."

The Prophet (صَلَّى ٱللَّهُ عَلَيْهِ وَسَلَّمَ) told Umm Sinān,

إِذَا جَاءَ رَمَضَانُ فَاعْتَمِـرِي، فَإِنَّ عُمْـرَةً فِيهِ تَعْدِلُ حَجَّةً -أَوْ قَالَ-: حَجَّةً مَعِي.

"When Ramaḍān comes, perform `Umrah because doing so equals the performance of Hajj; (or he said: Hajj with me)."

In short, performing an `Umrah in Ramaḍān is equal in reward to performing a Hajj with the Prophet (صَلَّىٱللَّهُعَلَيْهِوَسَلَّمَ). *[60]

[60] This part is taken from a Friday sermon delivered on Ramaḍān 15th 1433 / 8/3/2012. It is titled, "How to live Ramaḍān?".

BE GRATEFUL TO THE FAVORS OF ALLĀH IF YOU ARE ALIVE DURING THIS BLESSED MONTH

Fellow Muslim, Allāh (تَبَارَكَ وَتَعَالَى) blessed you with life during this month [of Ramaḍān]. Accordingly, it would be best if you spent a considerable time deliberating in reflection to capture the plentiful forms of mercy Allāh bestows during that month. Remember the origin and reason for our creation. Allāh (جَلَّ وَعَلَا) said:

﴿ وَمَا خَلَقْتُ ٱلْجِنَّ وَٱلْإِنسَ إِلَّا لِيَعْبُدُونِ ﴿٥٦﴾ ﴾

"I created jinn and mankind only to worship Me." [Sūrah adh-Dhaariyaat (51):56]

Al-Nawawī (رَحِمَهُ ٱللَّهُ) commented:

وَهَذَا تَصْرِيحٌ بِأَنَّهُمْ خُلِقُوا لِلْعِبَادَةِ، فَحُقَّ عَلَيْهِمُ الْاِعْتِنَاءُ بِمَا خُلِقُوا لَهُ، وَالْإِعْرَاضُ عَنْ حُظُوظِ الدُّنْيَا بِالزَّهَادَةِ؛ فَإِنَّهَا دَارُ نَفَادٍ لَا مَحَلُّ إِخْلَادٍ، وَمَرْكَبُ عُبُورٍ، لَا مَنْزِلُ حُبُورٍ، وَمَشْرَعُ انْفِصَامٍ، لَا مَوْطِنُ دَوَامٍ.

"This verse contains an unequivocal declaration that they are created for the sole purpose of worship. Therefore, they must pay sufficient care because they are created for and shun worldly gains since it will vanish. None is

immortal in this world because it is merely a passing and has never been an eternal residence."[61]

Reflect deeply on the favors Allāh bestowed upon you, for:

﴿ وَإِن تَعُدُّوا۟ نِعْمَتَ ٱللَّهِ لَا تُحْصُوهَآ ٣٤ ﴾

"if you attempt to count to the blessings of Allāh, you could never calculate them." [Sūrah ʾIbrāhīm (14):34]

The tremendous favor of Allāh is being a Muslim. Countless people on this earth do not testify that there is no deity worthy of worship but Allāh. Indeed, it is a favor from Allāh, and He bestows it on whomever He wills. I praise Allāh Almighty for guiding us to Islām since many people are affiliated to it, though they disobey its instructions either publicly or privately. They are neglectful of their obligations and are drowned by their own sins and indulgences. On the other hand, you are engrossed by the favors of Allāh Almighty such that you live off His generous sustenance and have a healthy body. In return, you must be grateful to Him verbally and in practice.

One of the most expressive means of gratefulness is to obey Allāh Almighty and refrain from His prohibitions because His favors last as much as one's degree of gratitude, as He (جَلَّ وَعَلَا) said:

﴿ لَئِن شَكَرْتُمْ لَأَزِيدَنَّكُمْ ﴾

"If you are thankful, I will give you more." [Sūrah ʾIbrāhīm (14):7]

Another favor from Allāh is keeping you alive until you reached the month of Ramaḍān, as death has overtaken many close friends.

[61] Riyāḍ al-Ṣāliḥīn: 27.

Therefore, you must seize this opportunity to increase your record of good deeds and draw yourself much closer to Allāh, the Lord of the worlds. Be stringent with your time so as not waste it. Remember those who fasted and prayed Eid alongside us last year; now, they are long dead. Seize as many opportunities as possible and heed the Prophet's (ﷺ) advice:

اغْتَنِمْ خَمْسًا قَبْلَ خَمْسٍ: حَيَاتَكَ قَبْلَ مَوْتِكَ، وَصِحَّتَكَ قَبْلَ سَقَمِكَ، وَفَرَاغَكَ قَبْلَ شُغْلِكَ، وَشَبَابَكَ قَبْلَ هِرَمِكَ، وَغِنَاكَ قَبْلَ فَقْرِكَ.

"Take advantage of five before five: your life before death, your health before ailment, your leisure time before work, and your youthfulness before old age and your wealth before poorness."[62]

Al-Ḥākim records it, and al-ʾAlbānī graded it as sound.

May Allāh have peace and blessings upon our Prophet Muḥammad, his family, and his Companions. *[63]

---

[62] Recorded by ibn abū al-Dunyā in 'Qiṣar al-ʾAmal' as part of his Hadith encyclopedia: (5/58) no. (111), al-Ḥākim in ʾal-Mustadrakʾ: (4/306) no. (7846), and al-Bayhaqī in ʾShuʿab al-ʾĪmānʾ: (12/476) no. (9767) on the authority of ibn ʾAbbas (may Allāh be pleased with him).
Al-Ḥākim graded this hadith as sound and good (ḥasan ṣaḥīḥ). It is also graded as sound by Al-ʾAlbānī in ʾṢaḥīḥ al-Targhīb wa al-Tarhībʾ: (3/311) no. (3355). It is reported on the authority of ʾAmr ibn Maymūn al-ʾAwdī in a Mursal form. Check ʿʾShuʿab al-ʾĪmānʾ: (12/476-478).

[63] This part is taken from a Friday sermon delivered on Ramaḍān 2nd 1436 / 6/19/ 2015. It is titled "Purifying the heart in Ramaḍān".

APPENDIX: STRIVE TO THAT WHICH IS BENEFICIAL TO YOU

In the name of Allāh, the Most Gracious, the Most Merciful

All Praise is due to Allāh; we praise Him, seek His help, and His forgiveness. We seek Allāh's refuge from the evils of ourselves and the evil consequences of our deeds. Whoever Allāh guides, no one can lead astray. Whoever Allāh leads astray, no one can guide. I testify that none has the right to be worshiped, but Allāh, the One, has no partners with Him. I testify that Muḥammad is His servant and Messenger; peace and blessings be upon him.

﴿ يَٰٓأَيُّهَا ٱلَّذِينَ ءَامَنُواْ ٱتَّقُواْ ٱللَّهَ حَقَّ تُقَاتِهِۦ وَلَا تَمُوتُنَّ إِلَّا وَأَنتُم مُّسۡلِمُونَ ١٠٢ ﴾

"O you who believe! Fear Allāh (by doing all that He has ordered and by abstaining from all that He has forbidden) as He should be feared. [Obey Him, be thankful to Him, and remember Him always], and die not except in a state of Islam (as Muslims) with complete submission to Allāh." [Sūrah ʿĀli ʿImrān (3):102]

﴿ يَٰٓأَيُّهَا ٱلنَّاسُ ٱتَّقُواْ رَبَّكُمُ ٱلَّذِى خَلَقَكُم مِّن نَّفْسٍ وَٰحِدَةٍ وَخَلَقَ مِنْهَا زَوْجَهَا وَبَثَّ مِنْهُمَا رِجَالًا كَثِيرًا وَنِسَآءً ۚ وَٱتَّقُواْ ٱللَّهَ ٱلَّذِى تَسَآءَلُونَ بِهِۦ وَٱلْأَرْحَامَ ۚ إِنَّ ٱللَّهَ كَانَ عَلَيْكُمْ رَقِيبًا ۝١ ﴾

"O mankind! Be dutiful to your Lord, Who created you from a single person (Adam), and from him (Adam) He created his wife [Hawwa (Eve)], and from them both He created many men and women and fear Allāh through Whom you demand your mutual (rights), and (do not cut the relations of) the wombs (kinship). Surely, Allāh is Ever an All-Watcher over you." [Sūrah An-Nisā' (4):1]

﴿ يَٰٓأَيُّهَا ٱلَّذِينَ ءَامَنُواْ ٱتَّقُواْ ٱللَّهَ وَقُولُواْ قَوْلًا سَدِيدًا ۝٧٠ يُصْلِحْ لَكُمْ أَعْمَٰلَكُمْ وَيَغْفِرْ لَكُمْ ذُنُوبَكُمْ ۗ وَمَن يُطِعِ ٱللَّهَ وَرَسُولَهُۥ فَقَدْ فَازَ فَوْزًا عَظِيمًا ۝٧١ ﴾

"O you who believe! Keep your duty to Allāh and fear Him, and speak (always) the truth. He will direct you to do righteous good deeds and will forgive you your sins. And whosoever obeys Allāh and His Messenger (ﷺ) he has indeed achieved a great achievement (i.e., he will be saved from the Hellfire and made to enter Paradise)." [Al-Ahzab: 70 – 71]

The most truthful speech is the Book of Allāh, and the best guidance is the guidance of Muḥammad; peace be upon him. The worst matters are the newly invented (in religion), every newly invented matter is an innovation, and every innovation is a heresy, and every heresy is in the Fire.

Imām Muslim collected in *Ṣaḥīḥ*[64] on the authority of Abu Hurayrah, may Allāh be pleased with him, the Messenger of Allāh, peace be upon him, said:

الْـمُؤْمِنُ الْقَوِيُّ خَيْرٌ أَحَبُّ إِلَى اللهِ مِنَ الْـمُؤْمِنِ الضَّعِيفِ، وَفِي كُلٍّ خَيْرٌ، احْرِصْ عَلَى مَا يَنْفَعُكَ، وَاسْتَعِنْ بِاللهِ، وَلَا تَعْجِزْ، وَإِنْ أَصَابَكَ شَيْءٌ؛ فَلَا تَقُلْ: لَوْ أَنِّي فَعَلْتُ؛ كَـانَ كَذَا وَكَذَا، وَلَـكِنْ قُلْ: قَدَرُ اللهِ وَمَا شَاءَ فَعَلَ؛ فَإِنَّ لَوْ تَفْتَحُ عَمَلَ الشَّيْطَانِ.

> **"A firm believer is better and dearer to Allāh than a weak one, and in both, there is good. Strive to that which is beneficial for you. Keep seeking Allāh's help, and do not fail to do so. If you are afflicted in any way, do not say: 'If I had taken this or that step, it would have resulted into such and such, 'but say only: 'this is Allāh's decree, and He did as He willed.' The word 'if' paves the way for satanic thoughts."**

<u>In this Hadith:</u>

The Prophet, peace be upon him, refers to many essential matters in the religion of Allāh (سُبْحَانَهُ وَتَعَالَى). In this noble Hadith, we first notice the rule stated by *Ahlu Sunnah Wal-Jama'ah,* which establishes that faith can increase and decrease. Some people have more religious

[64] *Ṣaḥīḥ Muslim*: (4/2052 No. 2664).

faith than others. Additionally, it can increase by doing righteous good deeds and decrease by doing evil deeds.

"The firm believer" firmness here refers to one's determination and ability to let the body obey Allāh Almighty rather than the body's strength, wellbeing, and health in the first place. It might be a test from Allāh (سُبْحَانَهُ وَتَعَالَىٰ). Those who use their power and fitness in doing evil deeds and doing wrong to others may fail.

However, **"the firm believer"** refers to one's determination which provokes them to seek useful knowledge, urges them to do righteous good deeds, and makes them worship Allāh (سُبْحَانَهُ وَتَعَالَىٰ) as their Lord and Master wills.

الْمُؤْمِنُ الْقَوِيُّ خَيْرٌ وَأَحَبُّ إِلَى اللهِ مِنَ الْمُؤْمِنِ الضَّعِيفِ

"**A firm believer is better and dearer to Allāh than a weak one**" in order not to think that the weak believer, who has the basis of faith and the reality of Islam with no urge to do righteous good deeds or striving towards all what is good and fails to do good deeds in the aftermath of a calamity, has not good in him at all, the Messenger, peace be upon him, said:

وَفِي كُلٍّ خَيْرٌ

"**and in both, there is good**." In other words, there is good in the firm believer and the weak one as well.

This common good aspect originates from the basis of faith. He is a believer even if he hardly does righteous good deeds to his benefit in life to come, including seeking knowledge, doing righteous good deeds, striving towards all that is good, and adhering to acts of worship.

الْمُؤْمِنُ الْقَوِيُّ خَيْرٌ وَأَحَبُّ إِلَى اللهِ مِنَ الْمُؤْمِنِ الضَّعِيفِ، وَفِي كُلٍّ خَيْرٌ

"A firm believer is better and dearer to Allāh than a weak one, and in both, there is good."

The Prophet (صَلَّى ٱللَّهُ عَلَيْهِ وَسَلَّمَ) continued:

احْرِصْ عَلَى مَا يَنْفَعُكَ

"**Strive to that which is beneficial for you**." this sentence is considered a pithiness of speech of the Messenger of Allāh (صَلَّى ٱللَّهُ عَلَيْهِ وَسَلَّمَ). It is a basis and a rule for Muslims. If one adheres to it, Allāh will rectify his affairs in this worldly life and the Hereafter.

اِحْرِصْ عَلَى مَا يَنْفَعُكَ

"**Strive to that which is beneficial for you**." Do not waste your energy. Do not waste your time. Do not squander your money. You should undoubtedly adhere to what is beneficial for you.

This makes one look deep inside the consequences, i.e., what will happen in the coming days. The believer can be farsighted, have foresight, and consider which affairs should be done and left behind rather than be short-sighted and unable to see far.

اِحْرِصْ عَلَى مَا يَنْفَعُكَ

"**Strive to that which is beneficial for you**." What is beneficial for one, in reality, is to know his Lord, his Gracious Names and Attributes, and believe in and practice the revelation with which the infallible Prophet, peace be upon him, was sent.

One should know what the Prophet (صَلَّى ٱللَّهُ عَلَيْهِ وَسَلَّمَ) was sent with and then turn it into a belief, words, and actions. Many people are granted a piece of knowledge by Allāh Almighty. In reality, this knowledge is valuable, but to him, it is of no use.

The Prophet (صَلَّى ٱللَّهُ عَلَيْهِ وَسَلَّمَ) indicated that the one who encourages people to do good deeds but does not is compared to a candle burning by itself to give light to others. This is the case for the one who gains a piece of knowledge or gives Daʿwah to let ones worship the Lord of the worlds, but he does not practice what he says, as stated by the Prophet (صَلَّى ٱللَّهُ عَلَيْهِ وَسَلَّمَ). Reported Usamah Ibn Zayd, (رَضِيَ ٱللَّهُ عَنْهُ), the Prophet (صَلَّى ٱللَّهُ عَلَيْهِ وَسَلَّمَ) said:

يُؤْتَى بِالرَّجُلِ يَوْمَ الْقِيَامَةِ، فَيُلْقَى فِي النَّارِ، فَتَنْدَلِقُ أَقْتَابُ بَطْنِهِ، فَيَدُورُ بِهَا كَمَا يَدُورُ الْحِمَارُ بِالرَّحَى، فَيَجْتَمِعُ إِلَيْهِ أَهْلُ النَّارِ، فَيَقُولُونَ: يَا فُلَانُ مَا لَكَ؟ أَلَمْ تَكُنْ تَأْمُرُ بِالْمَعْرُوفِ وَتَنْهَى عَنِ الْمُنْكَرِ؟ فَيَقُولُ: بَلَى، قَدْ كُنْتُ آمُرُ بِالْمَعْرُوفِ وَلَا آتِيهِ، وَأَنْهَى عَنِ الْمُنْكَرِ وَآتِيهِ.

"A man will be brought on the Day of Resurrection and thrown into the Fire, and his intestines (*Aqtab*[65]) will slip out. He will go around by them as a donkey goes around a millstone. The dwellers of Hell will gather around him and say: 'So-and-so, what is the matter with you? Did you not use to command us to do right and forbid us from doing wrong?' He will reply: 'Yes, I commanded you to do right,

[65] *Aqtab* means entrails and intestines. *Indilaq* means to come out. See *Sharh An-Nawawi* upon *Ṣaḥīḥ Muslim* (18/118-119)

but I did not do it myself, and I forbade you from doing wrong, but I did it myself." It is collected in two *Ṣaḥīḥ*[66].

According to the Noble Qur'ān, the Prophet (صَلَّى ٱللَّٰهُ عَلَيْهِ وَسَلَّمَ) warned about words without actions.

اِحْرِصْ عَلَى مَا يَنْفَعُكَ

"**Adhere to that which is beneficial for you**." Try your hardest to know the beginning of the path. We are born and raised based on the knowledge of the society we are born in. This knowledge is not clear from what corrupts the origin, such as impurities and so forth.

How many irreligious beliefs are held by people for which Allāh has sent down no manifest authority!!

Many creeds, related to the unseen and the like, concern which people believe in what is not loved or accepted by Allāh. Conversely, they believe in what is contrary to what the Messenger of Allāh (صَلَّى ٱللَّٰهُ عَلَيْهِ وَسَلَّمَ) was sent with.

They took these dogmas from those around them in their societies. In reality, they are major innovations in one's belief system. It is awfully horrible. You often hear words like salat, for instance, is not of great value like the genuineness of the heart and good-heartedness!!

Many people say: everything is of no use as long as the heart is pure and good. Additionally, they may mock those who perform salat.

[66] *Ṣaḥīḥ Al-Bukhari*: (6/331, No. 3267), *Ṣaḥīḥ Muslim*: (4/2290, No. 2989). In the narration of Al-Bukhari: (13/48, No. 7098): "A man will be brought and thrown into the fire. He will go around by them like a donkey goes around a millstone. The dwellers of Hell will gather around him and say: 'So-and-so! Did you not use to command us to do right and forbid us from doing wrong? …" so he referred to a close narration.

For instance, they say: "You offer salat and commit sins." Supposedly, this does not lead to dispraising salat itself. Many people offer acts of worship but do not rectify their behavior. Supposedly, this does not lead to dispraising this act of worship, but it dispraises those who offer it.

Those people resort to such beliefs: indeed, this act of worship does nothing with one's faith in the heart or creed, including purity, sincerity, chastity, clarity, and its likes! It is totally wrong.

No one should underestimate good-heartedness. No one can be saved without good-heartedness. Whoever comes to Allāh with a heart free (from evil) will be saved.

A heart can be pure by clearing polytheism, innovation, bad morals such as envy, malice, hatred, cheating Muslims, and the like.

All these are diseases of the heart that can make it sick if rooted in the heart. No one should underestimate the matter of the purity of the heart.

However, doing good deeds is an integral part of the faith. Faith includes words and actions, a belief in the heart, a saying of the tongue, and actions of the body.

So salat is an integral part of faith, and Zakat is an essential part of faith. In a Hadith collected by Muslim, the Prophet, peace be upon him, frankly stated:

الْإِيمَانُ بِضْعٌ وَسِتُّونَ -أَوْ: وَسَبْعُونَ- شُعْبَةً، أَدْنَاهَا إِمَاطَةُ الْأَذَى عَنِ الطَّرِيقِ، وَأَعْلَاهَا قَوْلُ: لَا إِلَهَ إِلَّا اللهُ، وَالْحَيَاءُ شُعْبَةٌ مِنَ الْإِيمَانِ.

"Faith consists of sixty-odd or seventy-odd branches, the lowest of which is the removal of what is injurious from the road, the most excellent of which is the declaration that

none has the right to be worshipped, but Allāh; and modesty is a branch of faith."[67]

In this noble Hadith, the Prophet (ﷺ) stated that faith is a belief in the heart, a saying of the tongue, and actions of the limbs. The Prophet, peace be upon him, said:

الْإِيمَانُ بِضْعٌ وَسِتُّونَ -أَوْ: وَسَبْعُونَ- شُعْبَةً، أَدْنَاهَا إِمَاطَةُ الْأَذَى عَنِ الطَّرِيقِ

"Faith consists of sixty-odd or seventy-odd branches, the lowest of which is the removal of what is injurious from the road."

It is an action. If one noticed a thorny branch, stone, or something detrimental to the passers-by in the road, they should set it aside.

The Prophet (ﷺ) clarified the importance of this good deed. So he, peace be upon him, said:

بَيْنَمَا رَجُلٌ يَمْشِي بِطَرِيقٍ، وَجَدَ غُصْنَ شَوْكٍ عَلَى الطَّرِيقِ، فَأَخَّرَهُ، فَشَكَرَ اللهُ لَـهُ، فَغَفَرَ لَـهُ.

"While a man was going on a road, he saw a thorny branch and removed it from the road. So Allāh was pleased by his action and forgave him."[68]

---

[67] Collected by Muslim in *Ṣaḥīḥ*: (1/63, No. 35). It is also collected in *Ṣaḥīḥin*: *Ṣaḥīḥ Al-Bukhari* (1/51, No. 9) and *Ṣaḥīḥ Muslim*: (1/63, No. 35) with the narration of "Faith is seventy-odd [according to Al-Bukhari: sixty] branches and modesty is a branch of faith."

[68] Collected by Al-Bukhari in *Ṣaḥīḥ*: (2/139, No. 652) and Muslim in *Ṣaḥīḥ*: (4/2021, No. 1914) as reported by Abu Huraira, may Allāh be pleased with him.

Removal of harm from the road, which is done by the body parts, is a part of faith.

لَا إِلَـهُ إِلَّا اللهُ

"**None has the right to be worshipped, but Allāh**" is indeed said by the tongue and the heart.

This is a tongue saying, and that is the action of the body parts. "**Modesty,** as one of the deeds of the heart**, is a branch of faith**."

In this mutually agreed authentic Hadith, the Prophet, peace be upon him, stated that faith is a belief in the heart, a saying of the tongue, and action of the limbs.

Many people separate one's deeds away from the meaning of true Islamic faith; it is a baseless innovation in belief. The scholars called this innovation *Irja'*. One can be a *Murji'* exceeding the limits in *Irja'* while he is ignorant of what is *Irja.'* He is unaware that he is involved in a major act of innovation in true Islamic belief that distorts Islam's great religion.

One utters words that they believe according to what they learned from society and those who taught religion. They do not warn him about these evil beliefs and do not clarify the creed of *Ahlu-Sunnah*. So they get involved in *Irja'*.

In another narration of Muslim, "When one saw a thorny branch on a road, he said: By Allāh! I will remove this injurious thing from the road of Muslims, so he entered Paradise." In another narration, "I have seen a man luxuriated in Paradise due to cutting a tree, in the middle of a road, injurious to the people." This Hadith is narrated by Abu Barzah, may Allāh be pleased with him, in *Ṣaḥīḥ Muslim*.

Unconsciously, many people are found to be determinist also in belief. Even if you said to him: "you are a determinist person," he could not grasp what you say.

Many people commit evil deeds, but they argue that they do it by Allāh's will. One commits sins, but if they are to blame, they say: "Allāh forced me to do that." So he argues that the divine decree is a reason behind committing sins and doing evil deeds.

Divine Decree is one of the pillars of faith. One should believe in Divine Decree. No belief can be validated without it. It is the sixth pillar of faith in the great religion of Islam. No one can argue that Divine Decree is a reason behind doing evil deeds. In other words, when one sins, he commits it at will according to the will of Allāh (سُبۡحَانَهُۥوَتَعَالَىٰ); although it is of his own free will.

Optionally speaking, the sins are committed, and the righteous good deeds are done by the servant's choice and thanks to Allāh's Grace,

﴿ وَٱلَّذِينَ ٱهۡتَدَوۡاْ زَادَهُمۡ هُدٗى وَءَاتَىٰهُمۡ تَقۡوَىٰهُمۡ ١٧ ﴾

> **"While as for those who accept guidance, He increases their guidance, and bestows on them their piety."** [Sūrah Muḥammad (47):17]

If one is granted the general guidance, Allāh will bestow upon them the unique guidance by Allāh's Grace and Assistance and discernment of his religious affairs to be more determined to do righteous good deeds.

Everyone should believe in Divine Decree, but no one should claim that it is the reason behind committing sins. It should be arguably mentioned in case of distresses. In other words, if one is afflicted with a calamity and suffers a tragic fate, he shall say, as stated in the said Hadith:

قَدَرُ اللهِ وَمَا شَاءَ فَعَلَ

"This is Allāh's decree, and He did what He willed."

So Allāh sends down His tranquillity upon their heart. They also should know that this calamity cannot be avoided anywise. It is a decree established by Allāh Almighty to test them.

Many people argue that the Divine Decree is the reason behind committing these sins and utter words known by the old and the young, the learned and the ignorant. They also claim that what is written on one's forehead will never fail.

If one means what is relevant to Divine Decree only, it will never fail. However, if it is used as an argument against one's Lord to commit sins and offenses, it will be rejected.

The Messenger of Allāh (صَلَّى ٱللَّهُ عَلَيْهِ وَسَلَّمَ) said:

وَفِي كُلٍّ خَيْرٌ، احْرِصْ عَلَى مَا يَنْفَعُكَ

"and in both, there is good. Strive to that which is beneficial for you."

Learn the matters of religion. Adhere to the rulings of belief. Belief must be based on an original fundamental you knew and learned from the Book of Allāh and your Prophet's Sunnah.

It would help if you tried your hardest to learn it. Many people ignore it even if they are highly certified and obtain high degrees in many branches of science, whether relevant to Sharia or not.

So, if you asked someone: what is the first obligation upon the one in this life? What is the last obligation upon the one at the end of their life?

The first and last obligation is:

أَشْهَدُ أَلَّا إِلَـهَ إِلَّا اللهُ

"**None has the right to be worshipped but Allāh**." So, the first obligation is to bear a truthful testimony.

To testify that none has the right to be worshipped except Allāh alone and that Muḥammad is the Messenger of Allāh is the first obligation upon the servant.

Also, it is the last word one should utter when leaving this worldly life:

مَنْ كَـانَ آخِرَ كَلَامِهِ: لَا إِلَـهَ إِلَّا اللهُ؛ دَخَلَ الْـجَنَّـةَ.

> **"Whoever dies with the last words (whose meaning is): "There is none has the right to be worshipped but Allāh" will enter Paradise."[69]**

So "There is none has the right to be worshipped, but Allāh" is the first and last obligation and what is between them.

If you asked a Muslim: "What is the meaning of '***La Ilaha Illa Allāh***'?"

---

[69] Collected by Abu Dawud in *As-Sunan*: (3/190, No. 3116) reported by Moadh Ibn Jabal, may Allāh be pleased with him.
This Hadith is graded as *Hassan* by Al-Albani in *Irwa' Al-Ghalil*: (3/149, No. 687).

The answers will be different. Some will reply: "***'La Ilaha Illa Allāh'*** means **'no Creator but Allāh.'**"

If this is the correct answer, ***'La Ilaha Illa Allāh'*** will not be mentioned in this Good Word but "No Lord but Allāh"!!

Here it refers to Allāh's worship rather than lordship. '***La Ilaha***' means none has the right to be worshipped. '***Illa Allāh***' but Allāh, the Lord of the worlds.

If you asked a Muslim about the Good Word; - which if they believed in but went to Hellfire in which they dwelt to receive punishment for what they committed by one's hands, to be cleansed to join the righteous ones in the home of the pure, honest people, the Garden of Eternity, if this word accompanies one, but they went and dwelt in Hellfire for some time, - they will have to find a way out of the Hellfire one day.

Whoever believes in "*La Ilaha Illa Allāh*" will not dwell in the Hellfire eternally.

A great deal of Muslims does not know the meaning of this Great Word. So, if you asked them, they would say: "No Creator except Allāh. No Lord except Allāh."

Some say: 'the command is for none except Allāh.'

All these are in the wrong direction.

'***La Ilaha Illa Allāh***' means none has the right to be worshipped but Allāh.

Why must we say: 'none has the right to be worshipped?

Because if we do not say **"has the right"** but we state that "***La Ilaha Illa Allāh***" means none is worshipped but Allāh, we will compare

Allāh Almighty to all the worshipped gods because there are many gods worshipped besides Allāh.

In some religions, human beings are worshipped. In India, the cows are worshipped by Hindus and other groups. Additionally, in central Africa, idols are still worshipped besides Allāh (سُبۡحَانَهُۥوَتَعَالَىٰ).

The vain desire is also worshipped besides Allāh Almighty. It is obeyed against the command of Allāh (سُبۡحَانَهُۥوَتَعَالَىٰ). It is followed against the command of Islamic legislation.

﴿ أَفَرَءَيۡتَ مَنِ ٱتَّخَذَ إِلَٰهَهُۥ هَوَىٰهُ ﴾

> **"Have you seen him who takes his own lust (vain desires) as his *ilāh* (deity)?"** [Sūrah Al-Jāthiyah (44): 23]

So, his own vain desire turned out to be his deity besides Allāh.

All these are false deities worshipped besides Allāh. Many gods worshipped in this worldly life, but none of these said deities has the right to be worshiped. He is Allāh alone, '***La Ilaha Illa Allāh,***' i.e., none has the right to be worshipped but Allāh.

There is another noteworthy aspect, i.e., when you say: "none has the right to be worshipped," you will refer to worship. So, what is meant by worship?

You see, many kindhearted Muslims eagerly love doing good deeds with no authentic knowledge sought. They are not guided to what is beneficial for them in the worldly life and the life to come; the belief and faith matters come first.

If you say to a kind person, with a seemingly righteous appearance, tends to do righteous good deeds and abstain from evil acts: what is meant by worship? He cannot provide a clear definition of it. He will let it include some matters of worship and unknowingly leave out many issues relevant to worship.

In other words, he will say: 'worship includes prayer, *Sawm*, Zakat, and Hajj.' He will refer to these pillars, pillars of Islam, as the worship itself and nothing else.

It is a terrible mistake that lets one miss out on many righteous good deeds. Worship means everything Allāh loves and wills, including visible and invisible sayings and actions.

If one considered this definition adopted by the scholars, may Allāh have mercy upon them, they would know that one's whole life, even one's sleep, even when having intercourse with one's wife, one's food, drink, silence, speaking, movement, action, and sloth can be regarded as an act of worship to Allāh the Almighty provided one knows that it is an act of worship if Allāh, the Exalted, loves it.

Scholars, may Allāh have mercy upon them, say:

الْعِبَادَةُ: كُلُّ مَا يُـحِبُّـهُ اللهُ وَيَرْضَاهُ مِنَ الْأَقْوَالِ وَالْأَعْمَالِ الظَّاهِرَةِ وَالْبَاطِنَـةِ.

"Everything Allāh loves and wills, including visible and invisible sayings and actions."

'Invisible actions' includes the belief in the heart, actions, and sayings. It also includes that the heart loves and hates, hopes, fears, and does many acts of the heart.

All of these are the most extraordinary acts of worship one should offer Allāh the Exalted. If one loves ones with Allāh, they associate partners with Allāh the Exalted. However, if one loves Allāh or for the sake of Allāh, it will be the most extraordinary acts of worship offered to Allāh.

So, consider these authentic pieces of information on the religion of Allāh the Exalted. It is easy, but no one has any real intention or urges to seek knowledge because true legislative knowledge is for men and only sought by them. Those who are effeminate do not like seeking knowledge and have no desire to do so though it is the way to salvation, happiness, and success in this worldly life and the life to come.

All these lessons related to this noble prophetic text are a pithiness of our Noble Prophet's speech; peace be upon him.

اِحْرِصْ عَلَى مَا يَنْفَعُكَ

"**Strive to what is beneficial for you,**" seek beneficial knowledge, and do righteous good deeds. Strive to have the intention of getting closer to Allāh in everything you do,

اللُّقْمَةُ يَضَعُهَا أَحَدُكُمْ فِي فِـي اِمْرَأَتِـهِ؛ لَهُ بِهَا صَدَقَـةٌ

"even if it were a morsel which you put in your wife's mouth.[70]"

الْكَلِمَةُ الطَّيِّبَـةُ صَدَقَـةٌ

---

[70] Collected by Al-Bukhari in "*As-Ṣaḥīḥ*": (1/136, No. 56) and Muslim in "*As-Ṣaḥīḥ*": (3/1250, No. 1628) on the authority of Saad Ibn Abū Waqqās that the Messenger of Allāh, peace be upon him, said: "You will be rewarded for whatever you spend for Allāh's sake even if what you put in your wife's mouth."
In another narration: "..., even if it were a morsel which you put in your wife's mouth."

"The good word is considered *Sadaqah*.[71]"

ابْتِسَامُكَ فِي وَجْهِ أَخِيكَ صَدَقَةٌ

"Your smile at your brother's face is *Sadaqah*.[72]"

To take water from your bucket to pour into your needy brother's bucket is *Sadaqah.* To help one mount their camel, carry them to their camel, or carry their possessions on it is *Sadaqah.*

All these are acts of worship because *Sadaqah* is only an act of worship. If one offers these acts of worship, many good deeds will be written for him in case of good intention. When one intends to make their food and drink, help them worship Allāh, help them earn a lawful living in this worldly life, help you stop begging, save your face, and provide their family, children, and whom you are obliged to provide.

If one considers food and drink in this manner, they will enjoy drinking and eating as if it were Allāh's favors and considering the excellent intention with which one did so. Thus they will have a reward.

---

[71] Collected by Al-Bukhari in "*As-Ṣaḥīḥ*": (6/132, No. 2989) and Muslim in "*As-Ṣaḥīḥ*": (2/699, No. 1009) on the authority of Abu Huraira that the Messenger of Allāh, peace be upon him, said: "For every bone of man's fingers and toes *sadaqa* must be given. Every day the sun rises if one judges between two men it is *sadaqa*; if one helps a man with his camel, loading or lifting his goods on it, it is *sadaqa*; a good word is *sadaqa*; every step one takes towards salat is *sadaqa*; and if anyone removes anything injurious from the road it is *sadaqa*."

[72] Collected by At-Tirmidhi in *Al-Jami'*: (4/339, No. 1956) on the authority of Abu Dharr, the Messenger of Allāh, peace be upon him, said: "to smile at your brother's face is *sadaqah*, …" … Al-Hadith.
The Hadith is graded as Hassan by Al-Albani in "*As-Ṣaḥīḥa*": (2/116, No. 572) and "*Ṣaḥīḥ At-Targhib Wat-Tarhib*": (2/581, No. 2321).

Additionally, the Prophet (ﷺ) referred to something we rarely think about. So, he said:

وَفِي بُضْعِ أَحَدِكُمْ صَدَقَةٌ

"and in man's sexual intercourse (with his wife), there is a *Sadaqah*."

"They said: "O Messenger of Allāh! Is there a reward for him who satisfies his sexual need among us?"

He said:

أَرَأَيْتُمْ لَوْ وَضَعَهَا فِي حَرَامٍ أَكَانَ عَلَيْهِ فِيهَا وِزْرٌ؟ فَكَذَلِكَ إِذَا وَضَعَهَا فِي الْحَلَالِ كَانَ لَهُ أَجْرٌ.

"You see, if he were to satisfy it with something forbidden, would it not be a sin on his part? Similarly, if he were to satisfy it legally, he should be rewarded."[73]

Glorified be the Supreme Bestower and the Preserver!!

All these are acts of worship offered to Allāh (تَبَارَكَ وَتَعَالَى). Every activity in life, visible or invisible, is an act of worship offered to Allāh (تَبَارَكَ وَتَعَالَى) provided that good intention is declared.

Those successful individuals turn their habits into acts of worship, and unsuccessful ones turn their worship into habits. In other words, when one offers salat but his intention is away from salat, and does

[73] Collected by Muslim in "*As-Ṣaḥīḥ*": (2/697, No. 1006) on the authority of Abu Dhar, may Allāh be pleased with him.

not consider the salat as prostration to Allāh and making oneself upright before Allāh. They turn the act of worship into a habit.

However, those successful individuals turn a habit into an act of worship. When people eat, drink, marry, and wear clothes according to the Islāmic legislation, their practices turn into acts of worship for the sake of Allāh, the Beneficent the Merciful, thanks to the good intention.

احْرِصْ عَلَى مَا يَنْفَعُكَ، وَاسْتَعِنْ بِاللهِ

"Strive to that which is beneficial for you. Keep seeking Allāh's help": seek the help of Allāh Alone **"and do not fail to do so."**

So, in *Surah Al-Fātihah*:

﴿ إِيَّاكَ نَعْبُدُ وَإِيَّاكَ نَسْتَعِينُ ۝٥ ﴾

"You (Alone) we worship": we worship none but You (Alone). **"and You (Alone) we ask for help (for each and everything)."** [Sūrah *Al-Fātihah* (1): 5]

We seek the help of none but You (Alone). The religion (of Islam) is based on these two rules, i.e., worshipping (Allāh Alone) and seeking Allāh's help.

<u>In this Hadith:</u>

احْرِصْ عَلَى مَا يَنْفَعُكَ، وَاسْتَعِنْ بِاللهِ، وَلَا تَعْجِزْ، وَإِنْ أَصَابَكَ شَيْءٌ.

> **"Strive to that which is beneficial for you. Keep seeking Allāh's help, and do not fail to do so. If you are afflicted in any way."**

In other words, when one does their best to seek something beneficial for them, to apply for a job, do business, and so on, Allāh does not want it to come true, but Allāh keeps such a likely evil thing away now and then. So no one can know the Wisdom of Allāh but He.

وَإِنْ أَصَابَكَ شَيْءٌ، فَلَا تَقُلْ: لَـوْ أَنِّي فَعَلْتُ؛ لَكَـانَ كَذَا وَكَذَا.

"If you are afflicted in any way," i.e., something undesirable, **"do not say: 'If I had taken this or that step, it would have resulted into such and such,'"**

This is an objection to what Allāh decreed. It is an illegal use of "If" as "If" is sometimes used as an objection to what Allāh decreed as stated in this noble Hadith.

لَـوْ أَنِّي فَعَلْتُ؛ لَكَـانَ كَذَا وَكَذَا.

"If I had taken this or that step, it would have resulted into such and such" it is sometimes used as an objection to Sharia and rulings

﴿لَوْ أَطَاعُونَا مَا قُتِلُوا﴾

> **"If only they had listened to us, they would not have been killed."** [Sūrah *'Āli 'Imrān* (3):168]

As the hypocrites said about the martyrs of *Uhud* battle, may Allāh be pleased with them.

Abdullah Ibn Ubai Ibn Saloul sided with a third of the army in *Uhud* battle. Many Companions of the Prophet, peace be upon him, were killed; seventy Companions were killed. So the hypocrites used to say:

﴿ لَوۡ أَطَاعُونَا مَا قُتِلُواْۗ ﴾

"If only they had listened to us, they would not have been killed."

It was an objection to Sharia. "If" here is used unlawfully.

It is also used for a complaint to what Allāh decreed:

لَـوْ أَنِّي فَعَلْتُ؛ لَكَـانَ كَذَا وَكَذَا.

'If I had taken this or that step, it would have resulted into such and such.

It is also used for considering the Divine Decree as a justification for committing sins:

﴿ لَوۡ شَآءَ ٱللَّهُ مَآ أَشۡرَكۡنَا وَلَآ ءَابَآؤُنَا ﴾

"If Allāh had willed, we would not have taken partners (in worship) with Him, nor would our fathers" [Sūrah Al-ʾAnʿām (6):148]

Here "If" is used as an objection to the Divine Decree by justifying committing sins.

However, suppose it is based on Sharia. In that case, it will be worship offered to Allāh, the Exalted. When one hopes to do something good without objection to the legislation or Divine Decree and use Divine Decree to justify committing sins and offenses, it will be permissible. The Messenger of Allāh (ﷺ) said:

لَوِ اسْتَقْبَلْتُ مِنْ أَمْرِي مَا اسْتَدْبَرْتُ؛ مَا سُقْتُ الْـهَدْيَ

"If I had formerly known what I came to know lately, I would not have brought the sacrificial animal with me."[74]

Because the Prophet (ﷺ) was a *Qarin* in the Farewell Hajj and brought the sacrificial animal, he was not allowed to end *Ihram* until Hajj. So he performs the *'Umrah* in the months of Hajj although the Prophet, peace be upon him, ordered the Muslim, who have not brought the sacrificial animal, to end their Ihram after *'Umrah* and perform Hajj *At-Tamattu'* to perform the many acts of worship, i.e., Hajj to the Noble House of Allāh.

He (ﷺ) said:

لَوِ اسْتَقْبَلْتُ مِنْ أَمْرِي مَا اسْتَدْبَرْتُ؛ مَا سُقْتُ الْـهَدْيَ

"If I had formerly known what I came to know lately, I would not have brought the sacrificial animal with me."

i.e., I would have performed Hajj *At-Tamattu,'* and I would not have been a *Qarin*; peace be upon him.

Thus, this is permissible.

لَا تَقُلْ: لَـوْ؛ فَإِنَّ (لَـوْ) تَفْتَحُ عَمَلَ الشَّيْطَانِ.

"Do not say: 'If' because the word 'if' paves the way for satanic thoughts." It makes one worried and confused.

---

[74] Collected by Al-Bukhari in "*As-Ṣaḥīḥ*": (13/218, No. 7229) and Muslim in "*As-Ṣaḥīḥ*": (2/879, No. 1211) on the authority of A'isha, may Allāh be pleased with her.

"What no one knew but Allāh, do not busy yourself with" what Allāh the Exalted knew only, forget about it.

There are two types of patience: the patience of the noblemen and that of lowly individuals.

The noblemen are heartily satisfied with the Decree of Allāh upon them; with their tongue, they express their pleasure with their Lord the Exalted. They do not anger the Almighty Lord with their body parts with anything like slapping one's cheeks, tearing one's clothes, and plucking one's hairs.

Additionally, the tongue must utter no word but what pleases Allāh the Exalted:

إِنَّا للهِ وَإِنَّا إِلَيْهِ رَاجِعُونَ، اللَّهُمَّ أْجُرْنِي فِي مُصِيبَتِي، وَأَخْلِفْ لِي خَيْرًا مِنْهَا.

> **"We belong to Allāh and to Him shall we return; O Allāh, reward me for my affliction and give me something better than it in exchange for it."[75]**

It is not permissible to say: O what a great man he was! And so on … as an objection to what Allāh decreed.

So, one should strive to have the patience of the noble.

---

[75] Collected by Muslim in "*As-Ṣaḥīḥ*": (2/631, No. 918) on the authority of Umm Salama who said: I heard the Messenger of Allāh, peace be upon him, saying: "If any Muslim suffers a calamity says what Allāh ordered him to say:" We belong to Allāh and to Him shall we return; O Allāh, reward me for my affliction and give me something better than it in exchange for it," ' Allāh would give him something better than it in exchange." … the Hadith.

As for the lowly ones' patience, one must forget his late person even after a while.

It is an instinct which Allāh rooted in his creatures without which people cannot live on earth.

Times of sorrow come to an end throughout nights, days, and years. Every calamity fallen upon the servant is forgotten later. However, one should exercise the patience of the noblemen.

Those who exercise the ignoble men's patience will unwillingly forget it, they cannot remain sad to death, but their sorrow will gradually decrease.

So, strive to what is beneficial for you and your late person.

I supplicate Allāh to keep him firm when reckoning and forgive his sins.

May Allāh send his prayers and peace upon our Prophet, Muḥammad and his family, and Companions!

This sermon was delivered on Monday, December 4th, 2017, corresponding to Rabe' Al-Awwal 4th of 1438 AH.

Made in the USA
Middletown, DE
05 May 2021

38532184R00057